"The more you understand, the more you love; the more you love, the more you understand."

Thích Nhất Hạnh

For my parents, Pat and Jack, with love and gratitude

Real Lives
of
Married People

Stories by
Deirdre Mendoza

Content

Even Greatness Started Small
Los Angeles, 1988
9

Real Lives of Married People
Los Angeles, 2006
37

For All You've Done
Palm Springs, 2008
65

Condo in Redondo
Los Angeles, 2009
85

Whisper Language
Los Angeles, 2008
109

Even Greatness Started Small
Los Angeles, 1988

Within minutes they had skipped the formalities and were seated at the kitchen table of Dave's 1950s ranch-style house in Studio City, drinking a cup of hot, chamomile tea and picking at a pizza from Trader Joe's. Dave, who Alana and her roommate soon nicknamed *The Spritz*, explained that this job— should she choose to accept it—was more than just a job. It was potentially a life-changing experience, a crack at screenwriting in the trenches—with a pro. He pointed to an award on his desk, and whipped out a card from his wallet. It had three letters, *W.G.A.,* etched like a battle scar. Dave Spritzer was a card-carrying member of the Writer's Guild of America, a chosen one, who had continued to write comedies through a decade of political turmoil and into the next.

I had a partner, Mike, you see, and we were the shit—the young guys who wrote the comedy hits for stars like Burt and Goldie, you know—and then it all went south when Mike married his 'D'-girl, development girl, and started a partnership with her. You see this? Spritz asked.

Spritz held up an aging issue of *Variety*. First-look deal at the studio. Megabucks. Hey, I say good for them, man. Writing teams either self-destruct or age like a good Merlot.

Spritz pointed to a framed black and white photo on his shelf. Yup, that's Mike and me with Burt. Whoa! What a head of hair I had back then! We once blew a joint in Burt's trailer the size of a cannon. He knew the script was that good. We were all gonna make some bread.

Spritz chuckled. He was far away, reminiscing with Burt and the gang.

I can write, you know, Alana said, as she put her bag down on the table. I published a story in a pretty good journal and I wrote a couple of screenplays in college, so.

Spritz nodded his approval.

Alana continued. The lady at the agency says you're looking for someone who can be your right hand. Is that…what you want?

Spritz ran his hands through his frizzy hair, and grinned with big, squared off teeth. I need someone who can look me in the eye and say this could be better. Or, you know, this is shit. So, you do have experience with screenwriting, Elaine?

It's *Alana*. With three "a's." Yeah, I have a script about a mother and her teenage daughter who witness a murder. Anyway, at college, a lot of people thought it was really original and—I don't know—I guess I'm showing—shopping—it around.

Women in jeopardy, huh? That's an easy sell, Spritz said. Are you funny at all? 'Cause I'm working on a romantic comedy here. A kind of Billy Wilder thing set on the campaign trail. Needs smart, snappy banter. Can you do banter?

Uh, yeah. Banter, Alana said.

Good. Good. Hey, here's the deal. When the strike is over—which should be, you know, soon—we can sell this thing. It can only help your career. If not, there's always stripping—that was a joke.

Funny, Alana said, unsure how funny the stripper thing really was.

You really think writing this script with you will help me in my career? I mean, will my name be on this one? Will I get what's it called, *credit*?

You're getting ahead of yourself, kiddo, Spritz said. Don't worry, I know people. I'll talk you up.

He walked over to his desk, a noir-ish looking brown number with sturdy legs, which took up most of what would have been his dining room, if he had lived with a woman. The house had built-ins, swivel

11

chairs, and a carpeted staircase leading to a bedroom she never wanted to imagine.

Yanking on the bamboo shade, Spritz peered out at the street, before switching on his honking IBM Selectric. He looked like a captain checking the weather before easing his skiff into the channel. *El Capitan Dave.* He started pacing the room, thinking of his first slug line, his big opening.

Alana wasn't sure if Spritz could even imagine how eager she was. She ached for this opportunity like a budding plant given a chance on someone's front porch.

So, Mr. Dave—.

Just Dave.

So, Just Dave, when do we start?

What, kiddo? As soon as you finish your pizza.

One night after work, Kate asked Alana to move out. Kate had met a musician in a punk band who had asked for a ride home after playing a gig at a local club. He'd given her a tape of his band, The Other Digit, they shared a burrito and it was on.

Oh, his band, yeah, they're *so* good, Kate gushed. A cross between Lou Reed and, and—I don't know—The Stranglers. And he's got all these punk records, and we ended up talking all night and doing shots at this party in this warehouse space downtown…I lost track of time. There's something about him. He's insane. I mean he's…compelling, you know? When we woke up in the morning, he played me this song he wrote and I was basically like, you should just move in. And I figured now that you've got this Hollywood job with this amazing screenwriter, I guess I thought you'd want your own place.

Alana found a pint-sized, one-bedroom bungalow in Silver Lake, just off Fountain, near Circus of Books, for $480 a month. It seemed like a lot, but if she could pick up a second job— maybe some catering—in addition to working for The Spritz, she might be able to swing it. She had six boxes of stuff, a guitar and some tapes. Within ten days she was set-up in a new city in a new neighborhood.

On Sundays, she splurged on *The New York Times*, watched movies at The Vista, and drank thick espressos and ate guava cream cheese cake at Tropical, a Cuban bakery. Worries about money were a constant.

Alana became friendly with the leather-clad S&M neighbors, Sal and Hobie. They were prop guys on feature films, who were in sync with their bald pates and mustaches. They traded lasagna recipes, gossiped about some of the local leather guys who hung out on the street outside the laundromat, and talked about pruning the prolific fig tree in their shared back yard. One time when Hobie was out of town, Sal, the younger one, knocked on Alana's door and asked for a ride to the hospital. He was having trouble breathing. She sat with Sal in the waiting room for hours and worked on a crossword puzzle. She was sure from the signs that Sal had AIDS, but they never named it. When Hobie got back to town, he dropped off flowers on Alana's doorstep.

She didn't like where things were going with AJ. He would show up in his rickety old Lancer late at night, and while she was in the kitchen making him a snack, he would take off his shirt. Their history was heavy with intimacies, including a stay at an ashram in Upstate New York, an abortion, and Basquiat sightings at their local breakfast place during a sweltering summer in a shared walk-up on Avenue A.

When she met AJ in New York, he was an actor who worked as a bike messenger. A playful, animated guy, he showed up with the contracts in his bag, and a stack of papers for the shipping manager at Alana's father's office to sign. He had the grace of his Jamaican mother, a dancer with Alvin Ailey in New

York, and the quick-talking charm of his father, an Irish studio musician, who lived in Chicago. He was lean and rebellious, long lashes, and a mouth that was fixed in a dimply grin.

In the beginning, she and AJ exchanged only a few words, especially if the pen didn't work, or the weather was painfully cold, which it was quite often. Once they talked about going to a concert at Irving Plaza. Alana looked forward to seeing his dreamy face and watching him from the sixth-floor window as he straddled his flashy ten-speed Peugeot, cutting through the breathing swarm of taxis and buses. A beautiful kid with a wool beanie featuring the company emblem, *CWM* (City Wide Messengers) in black, graffiti-style letters.

After a few months, AJ started telling her about the rest of his life. He had done *Twelfth Night* with a company on Mott Street. He'd also been cast in toothpaste and basketball shoe commercials. He was thinking about moving to L.A., but first needed more cash.

One afternoon, he arrived at rush hour looking kind of stressed. He spoke quickly in a hoarse voice, asking Alana if she wanted to have dinner at Vesulka, a place in the East Village. Yes, she said, she would like that very much.

At dinner, he said something about how she was a very interesting woman. He didn't elaborate, but he said he'd had several lovers, some older, some younger, and none were as *intense*—that was the word he used—as she was. He assured her that *intensity* was a good thing, yet he wasn't sure that he believed in one great love. He said people shouldn't attach themselves to other people, that expectations were dangerous and that love shouldn't become a form of ownership over time.

For Alana, marriage was still a concept, not something she was sure she wanted. Was she supposed to want it? Stan and June did the Sunday crossword puzzle together in bed every week like a religious ritual, and they both loved tennis and Broadway shows, and taking naps right after Stan got home from a long business trip. But they also said horrible, degrading things to each other—sometimes at the breakfast table. Besides, how could you ever be sure you picked the right person to live with forever?

AJ had again become part of the rotation in Alana's romantic life in L.A. There were others who spent the night, or rode off on Vespas, or walked lazily down the hill in their wrinkled shirts. And it mostly felt good to connect with new people, new bodies, new ideas about love and sex. Just when she thought she'd outgrown him, AJ would show up, announce that he couldn't spend the night because he had an audition the next day, or because he had to take care of this or that. They'd make love like two old friends—lazily, but with a nice, predictable pattern to it—and then he disappeared for weeks at a time.

Alana spent some days thinking of him, rewinding their past. She thought of the summer they spent on the ashram in New York: perfumed gardens that looked like Eden. The long single cots with the Himalayan blankets. The ancient sound of the chimes spread by the breeze. AJ had convinced her to come with just a few words. *An opportunity for self-discovery*. Transformation. *Can't ignore it*. And he was right. The months at The Center with AJ were among the best times they had together. Alana had just finished college, but this was AJ's higher education. They each found comfort in the long silences, the daily walks and meditations, the unanswerable questions, the long passages, daily recitations, read aloud to each other. AJ seemed to understand his place in the universe. He had desires like everyone else, but they never seemed to stifle him.

Alana went out five nights a week and dragged herself up and over the canyon to work at Spritz's house. She'd perk up a little, listening to *Morning Becomes Eclectic*, a radio show with a lot of cool, new music. But if she heard something mournful about women and their problems, something like Etta James, Tracy Chapman, or Sinead O'Connor, she was toast. She cried in her car, the safest place to cry, and kept the habit of weeping-while-driving all her life.

Alana's mother called to check on her every week. She often caught her early in the morning, drowsy and semiconscious. June blamed it on the move out West. She always asked if Alana was depressed, or if she wanted to come back home.

The stereo and all your records are still in you room, June said, like she was announcing a limited offer. You could come and go, you know, no questions asked—it's not a den yet.

Alana said, I just got here, Mom. I need more time.

June had a way of pleading without asking a question. It was hard to resist shutting her down. But Alana couldn't shut her down. Not yet. She still needed June. And she needed to know that June still needed her. The space between them was growing wider; the time difference on the two coasts seemed to act as a metaphor.

Your father sold to the surf shops out there, you know. He says California's where all the loose marbles roll.

Yeah, he told me that a few times.

Anyone interested in your script? June asked.

Alana got silent for a while. June had a way of getting her in a headlock over the phone.

While they talked, Alana thought about the night at the Italian place in New York when she told her parents she was going out to L.A.—for a while. June's angular face sank, she pushed her plate away, and started rifling around in her bag for a Winston. Alana didn't know one decision could hurt her mother so badly. But it had to. She was about to put a whole country between them.

After Alana moved to her own place, she kept in touch with Kate. They met up at The Formosa Café, holding court there for hours until they moved the party back to Kate's front steps or to Alana's backyard.

Alana went to the screenwriter's party in the Canyon with two other writers from USC: Ben, an aspiring composer, who grew up in Manhattan and had his dark comedy optioned, and Collin, a daytime stoner who made her laugh.

The screenwriter and his girlfriend introduced Alana to Alejandro, or *Alex* to his buddies. He had a pair of wire-rimmed glasses held together with gaffer's tape, and dark, shaggy hair that held traces of paint. They said he was doing these political cartoons and mash-up zines. He was smart and funny and Kate, who arrived late to the party, said she thought Alana *should try him.*

Alex talked about the animated films he'd made at art school. He sounded passionate, like art was part of him. Like he was somehow destined for greatness.

Ever heard of Cal Arts? he asked. I went there and it was really cool. I mean parts of it sucked, but we got to make a lot of art. It was liberating.

Alana was hesitant about Alex at first. He seemed a little tricky when it came to romance. She thought he was the kind who might pursue you and pursue you, and then forget to call after he'd finally made love to you for hours. But there was something beguiling about him. He had a big library of art books and shoeboxes full of tapes. He was open, full of theories and ideas. He shared a rundown place off Abbott Kinney with a roommate and Alana was surprised to hear him say he'd been to boarding school in Connecticut.

The monday after the screenwriter's party, Alana told Spritz the good news.

Someone really wants to read my script. Alana's eyes were big.

A producer? Spritz asked, nodding his head with approval.

An agent, I guess. An agent's assistant. She said she would pass it on to her boss who's like huge. She thinks it sounds commercial.

That's a start. Yep, that's a start, Spritz said.

He had picked up sandwiches from Jerry's Deli and was toying with his pickle.

Here, kiddo, he said, handing her a sandwich. He waved his big greenie in Alana's direction. Put some meat on your bones. You've gotta eat.

I'm thinking of going back to being a vegetarian, she said, but thanks.

Listen, there are a lot of folks who'll take advantage of you, take your precious ideas and make them their own. You got that? Spritz looked serious. Alana nodded. I mean, my friend Janie says that if her boss likes it, it's pretty much a done deal.

Yeah, well, just remember, it's not a done deal 'til it's done. I thought that I could count on Mike, my partner of 12 years, but I learned that legitimacy is all relative. Spritz raised his furry eyebrows for emphasis.

Right, Alana said, making a mental note to be more skeptical, less trusting. But not right away.

Spritz slipped off his sneakers and lined them up by the door in the hall. He moved them two inches forward, straightened one, stepped aside. Then he moved them a few inches to the left, and then back to their original spot. When he seemed satisfied with their coordinates, he walked back to the desk and rested his arm on Alana's shoulder.

I like to move around a lot, Spritz explained. I need to get loose, get in the writer's headspace. You'll get used to it. The truth is, writers have their idiosyncrasies. Not to compare, but you must know Hemingway weighed himself several times a day. Faulkner drank whiskey… I like to work in my socks.

When Alana had imagined working in Hollywood, she hadn't pictured it like this, quiet and strangely intimate. An older man in sports socks, pacing in his living room, a pencil between his teeth.

They were on their midday break in Spritz's kitchen. The workday followed a tight schedule, often mapped on yellow legal pads, that included lunch at noon and a brief afternoon hiatus for coffee and a doughnut. Spritz would announce if he was "losing steam," or if he "just didn't have the juices flowing" that day. And he'd put on a new song or rework some dialogue from a previous scene.

I was thinking about the end of the first act, Spritz said, looking through his cabinet for some mood music. He pulled a record from its sleeve. I think we need to end it on Arnie making a more heroic gesture, like offering to drive her to the plane or offering to spend the night.

Spend the night? What's heroic about that? she asked.

Well, she needs him on her side, right? said Spritz.

Yeah, but that's not a heroic gesture. That's weak. She's not this pathetic woman who can't get by on her own.

That's weak, said Spritz, mocking her. You think everything he does is *weak* or *lame*. He seemed tired of Alana's ragging on the protagonist, a young speechwriter for an incumbent senator who gets it on with an intern.

No, I don't. I just think you always assume that she's this frail, incompetent—
The Kinks song crept in:

...I believe that you and me last forever
Oh yeah, all day and nighttime yours, leave me never...

Spritz's soundtrack alternately alleviated and added to Alana's frustration with the script, and the daily debate about the characters—some of whom she cast as misogynists. She protested about some of the male characters—but not too much. After all, it was Spritz's script.

Look, kiddo, Spritz said one afternoon, you've got to learn to keep some of your personal problems out of the work. Writing may seem like fun and games, but it's not.

What the—what's that supposed to mean?

You've shown up half an hour late for the past two weeks, you leave early. Last week you didn't even call until the afternoon to say you weren't coming in. We've gotta be professional here, you know. This is work.

I know what it is. Okay? I know what this is.

Spritz looked mad. His lip was twitching.

Well, good, he said. Then I'd appreciate some—I don't know—cooperation.

Alana looked down. Maybe I do have some personal problems, okay? Maybe not everything's about eating frozen pizza and getting in the mood to write. Some of us are struggling just to get along here, you know. I'm probably pregnant, okay?

Spritz paused. Then he nodded. *Probably?*

He put his hands in his pockets and the two writers stared at each other purposefully for maybe the first time. His eyes were wide and droopy with heavy lids, brown pockets opening and closing. He was Dave Spritzer, a 46-year-old man from the Valley. He'd probably never gotten anyone pregnant. Or maybe he had. Maybe he had sired bundles of children with women of all stripes. Alana really didn't know him at all. But she knew him enough to feel his concern.

I'm thinking we should just start fresh tomorrow, Spritz said, taking charge of the ship.

Yeah, okay. You can just sign me out for half a day. Alana's voice was small.

Spritz lifted the needle off the record and the room emptied. He pretended to look for an album cover while Alana stood at the door.

He looked up. Let me know if I can, you know, do anything, Spritz said.

Cars were lining up on Ventura Boulevard, bullying each other at the freeway entrance. The sky was hazy, a dull sheen of sun and clouds. The mountains she used as markers to distinguish north and south had vanished from the backdrop. She took the canyon all the way, up and over the hill.

When she reached the other side of Laurel Canyon, a cop car pulled up and signaled her over. She gave the young officer her license. She would remember the incident years later, partly because the officer was handsome, precision groomed, prematurely grey. A young Richard Gere would have played him in the movie. He explained flatly that he'd first stopped her because of a broken taillight and had turned up a warrant for her arrest.

Fuck! She hadn't paid the ticket for the moving violation—she had rolled through a stop sign on a side street—hadn't been drunk—had been careless. It could be taken care of at the precinct if she had $500 in cash.

The cell smelled sour, like piss and cigarettes. It was tight in there. The guy in the opposing cell had a Rasta vibe, dressed in a tie-dyed tee shirt and baggy pants. He called out to her in a singsong voice.

How you doin' Skinny? Mister Leon at your service.

Alana gave him a false smile, unsure of jail etiquette.

You the big cheese I saw with the walkie-talkie on Venice Boardwalk. Am I right? he said.

She shook her head.

Sure I did. You're Rajah's girl, the one walkin' round like you own the goddamn place.

I don't think so, was all she could manage.

What's the matter, Cheerios? You don't like talking to people like me?

I do. Yeah, but I'm in jail right now, Alana reminded him, I'm not feeling too chatty.

And, from across the way, he hummed:

…for the rain is falling…

Later that night, a guard with M-shaped eyebrows and a gun came by with some cloudy Tang. Alana gulped it down hoping she would never have to pee it out in the metal toilet. About three hours later the same guard pried open the heavy door and slid her out of her cell. She warned that there would only be a couple of tries to reach someone who could post bail.

Face it, Alana thought, the whole month of June *was a disaster.* She'd been in a state of panic for weeks, worried she was pregnant, worried about her options. And then, as if she had willed it, she found a stain of blood on the bench where she had been sitting silently, holding back tears. That cherry-colored stain on the bench was enough to make her cry with relief. She let herself revel in this relief, but crying wasn't an option. How to pay the rent? How to sell the script? How to tell AJ that things weren't working out with their friendly arrangement?

As the hours passed, Alana listed a few people who might be able to spring her from jail, but she couldn't think of anyone who could come up with a few hundred in cash right away—except for one. She made some calls, enunciated carefully, spelling out her coordinates. She usually started with, Hi, It's Alana, and I really fucking need your help.

Anybody comin' down? the guard called out.

Not really, Alana whispered.

What if no one comes?

The guard shrugged. Nothin', she said.

Nothing?

Just county in the morning.

Hours passed in the cell, as Alana bit her nails down to the flesh, imagining a fate that included strip searches and bright orange jumpsuits, hairnets and menthol cigarettes clutched between sets of mismatched teeth, and shivs made from rusty razors and slim-toothed combs. She thought of scenes from women's prison movies, particularly the one with Ida Lupino playing a sadistic warden who mercilessly extracts a confession from a pregnant woman. She thought of the other young offenders who had sat comatose on the knife-scarred bench where she was seated, sipping their powdery drinks, hoping someone of this strange and luscious humankind would absolve them.

Hours later, Spritz stood at the front of the jail with a deli sandwich in his hand. He didn't smile when he saw Alana. He just motioned for her to come over to the desk where they returned Alana's belongings. He had already paid the bail.

It was nearly two in the morning and there were plenty of cars on the road. They tried the radio for a minute but neither of them was in the mood for George Michael, for Madonna, for "Tears of A Clown."

The city spoke for itself. Lit with neon, papered with billboards, cars jamming up the freeway. It didn't matter that it was early morning, traffic was a constant.

I picked up your message and split right away, Spritz said. I had this sandwich from Jerry's in the fridge and I've heard the cuisine ain't exactly top notch in there. I was actually going to stop at the sushi place on the Boulevard, but then I thought, that's crazy. She just wants to get the hell out of there.

Thanks, Alana said, biting into a ham and cheese on rye, mustard squirting on her cheeks. Really, thanks.

Dave shifted in his seat and put his hand on Alana's knee. He sat up tall, cleared his throat. I'm worried about you, kiddo. I think you need to get a better handle on your life.

I fucked up, Dave.

Dave nodded. Kept his eyes on the road.

He was a middle-aged guy, a screenwriter with some real credits, living in the Valley, who liked the pastrami on rye from Jerry's Deli. That's who he was.

What am I going to do? Alana asked. The question was faint, more like wincing out loud. Should I go back home? I mean, back to New York?

Dave took a long breath and exhaled through his nose.

How old are you? Twenty-three? The thing is you take yourself with you wherever you go.

Alana thought about it and decided that Dave was right. Leaving L.A. didn't make sense, at least not yet. She'd just arrived. She hadn't done whatever it was—the great thing—she was meant to do.

You know Mike and I wrote together for years and all that time he had a plan in his head, Dave said. He wanted more out of it than just some credits. He wanted a career, an identity out here. Saw himself as a big fish, you know? So each day he got up, had his coffee, sat on the john for a while and read the trades, and then got down to business. He was going somewhere. He wasn't playing. Look at him now. He's calling the shots.

Alana said, Yeah, but you're dedicated, too.

Now I am, Dave said, but it took a while. Doing the work is part of it, but I had to understand my own worth, my own talent. Now I think everything I write—shit, everything I do—is real important. That's the thing. You've got to figure out what you want, you know, and go for it. No hesitation.

Alana had her one burning question: Do you think I can make it as a writer?

Who knows? he shrugged. I'll tell you one thing I've learned—L.A.'s not for people in doubt. Even greatness started small.

As they pulled into Alana's driveway, she could see that Sal and Hobie still had their lights on. Night owls, those two. Alana thought of inviting Dave in for a beer or a snack to thank him.

It's late, she said, not sure how he would respond.

It's been a long night. Dave agreed. Past my bedtime.

I can see what I have in the fridge. Probably not much.

As they got inside the house, Alana felt anxious. Dave reached for her, bundling her in his arms.

She let him pull her closer, feeling his coarse cheeks, his rough sideburns. He smelled like manly soap. His voice was older than the voices of the guys she knew; he felt rougher. He exhaled with a kind of grunt. He stroked her hair, started to put his lips to her face, fingered the buttons on her shirt. And she was forced to really see him not as a boss, not as a writer in the Valley, not as a strange guy who came into her life through an agency, but as a man, a solitary man who wanted something from her. Had Dave been to jail? Had he known romantic love? Alana knew him—and she didn't. She didn't know what it was to have lived beyond the years of youth and uncertainty, to have tried things and failed, to have survived the painful disappointment—and to have forced yourself to try again.

Nothing's going to happen, okay? Alana managed.

She felt scared, and pained at having to say it. She tried not to cry.

Dave put his fingers to her lips. That's fine, he whispered. That's fine for now.

They stood in the entrance of Alana's bungalow and Dave held her for what seemed like a long time. Everything got very still. Alana could hear some traffic sounds bouncing off the Boulevard, but nothing else in motion.

Eventually, Dave pulled away. Okay, kiddo, he said, get some rest. See you Monday.

And off he went, a seasoned screenwriter making a second go of it with a romantic comedy set on a campaign trail, snaking his way down Hyperion Avenue, until his Volkswagen Rabbit was swallowed up in the Friday night jumble and hum of the city.

Alana undressed, threw her clothes on the thrift store chair in her bedroom where her cat was curled up, and listened to her messages. There was one from Janie, saying that her boss had read the script and wanted to meet with her, and another from Kate saying she was sorry, that she was worried about Alana, but she had to work a late shift. She hoped someone had come to Alana's rescue.

And there was a message from Alex, the artist guy from the screenwriter's party inviting her to the movies. She felt good when she heard his voice, though she didn't know they would eventually marry and raise a child together. She didn't know they would travel the world, starting with a honeymoon at Machu Picchu in Peru. She didn't know they would stand by each other's side when burying parents, or that they would grow apart, separate and eventually consider divorce. For now, she had a message on her machine about the new Bertolucci film. It was playing on the West Side and Alex wondered if she'd like to see it. He left his number slowly, spelling out the digits—748-7-3-1-6. And he said *ciao* at the end, instead of good-bye. She played that message back a couple of times, believing there was a promise of joy hidden inside it.

On Monday, Alana would start up again, retrieving her car from the city impound, signing some papers and pulling out of the lot. It would be an impossibly beautiful day in Los Angeles, temperatures in the mid-to-high seventies, a golden cast over the houses; clouds stretched thin like whiskers. Alana would apologize to Dave for being late, reticently blaming the traffic, or blaming the universe for making her late. Dave would shake his head and say, What do you feel like hearing? before putting on a warm up song to get rolling.

At lunch, Dave would heat up a frozen pizza, and offer a Dr. Brown's Cream Soda. Alana would work hard all day, helping another writer meet his vision. She would work until the day came to its logical conclusion. Then, she would jump into her beat-up Toyota and cruise down Ventura Boulevard—up, up and over the canyon—watching closely for people walking in the street, for helicopters, for coyotes. For signs of life.

Real Lives of Married People
Los Angeles, 2006

As the munchkin-sized players gathered for the kick-off in their bright yellow and orange uniforms, she motioned for Ryan to sit down beside her on the blanket parked on the sideline. He offered a sip of his coffee in gratitude and asked what she'd been up to.

Everything and nothing had happened in his absence, she thought. *Where to begin.* She spoke in elliptical phrases about the first grade pageant in which Clara sang, "This Land is Your Land," and about the ill health of her father, who seemed to be hanging on after a minor stroke. Finally, she told Ryan about how she and several staffers had been dumped by the *L.A. Times* as part of a series of lay-offs that had dismissed some of the veteran and hardest working reporters. It was a blow, she said, but she had already started to get calls for freelance work covering the industry.

Good thing entertainment coverage never goes out of style, she said. Someone's got to keep our little family afloat.

Alana's husband Alex waved from the other end of the field, where he had set up base camp with the other soccer dads. Having been a competitive player growing up in Europe, Alex was consumed by the kids' games. He cruised the field, filming action shots with the new digital camera they'd gotten from Alana's father, and coached Clara to become a striker.

Put your hand up and call for the ball, he instructed.

Go, Davis! Ryan yelled, as his handsome forward, a long-haired replica of himself as a child, broke away with the ball down the left side.

Defense, Galaxy! Alana called out, swept up momentarily in the match.

Soon her mind wandered from the confines of the soccer field. She thought of driving somewhere with Ryan. Maybe to a movie at the Sunset 5, or a dinner at an Indian place she liked in the neighborhood. She'd wear a short dress and steal some cherry-flavored lip-gloss from one of Clara's discarded goodie bags. They would share a couple of dishes: Chicken Vindaloo and somasas with raita. They'd drink an Indian beer and have a sweet dessert. Nothing fancy.

Jesus, did you see that? Ryan asked, pointing toward the goal. She's a fierce one, that Clara. That nearly went in. Luckily, our goalie is brilliant. Who is that kid? Is he the one with the Italian father?

Alana shot a prideful look down to Alex, whose hands were still up in the air as an exclamation. Good try, Clara! he called out, before moving down-field to meet the team.

When half-time approached, Davis screeched with delight as his father poured chilled water down his back. He ran to greet his mother, who appeared throught the gate of the rec center with Davis' three-year-old sisters in tow, and pawed her for a sports drink from the vending machine.

There they are, Ryan said, standing up with a half-salute to greet the twins and his wife. Double Trouble.

Hey guys, Janie said, pushing the stroller care-fully over a bumpy patch of grass. Remind me never to say yes to a birthday party that starts at 9:30 in the fucking morning.

Janie turned to Ryan. Did you get me a latte? Guess not.

Oh. I didn't think you'd be here until later—

Never mind, Janie muttered.

Alana found the exchange familiar: the slights and disappointments over a forgotten cup of coffee, an episode of a show that was watched ahead of schedule, a kiss that was never planted. She recognized Janie as belonging to the smart and sarcastic woman school. A graduate of USC primed for a job in industry, Janie could have launched a peace initiative or started a non-profit in another life. Instead, she raised the twins and ferried Davis to soccer matches while Ryan traveled the world on location with emerging directors.

Who's winning? Janie asked.

She then whipped her head around to end a high-pitched squabble between Kayla and her sister over a plush toy caterpillar. Girls, stop. Just stop, she said.

We're two-zip, our favor, said Ryan, But, he continued, no one keeps score in this league, right? The kids aren't focused on trivial things like winning or losing.

Janie hoisted Maggie, the fidgety, slightly larger twin, up on her hip, and asked Alana what they were doing later. We can offer cold beers, a shady back yard, and a kiddie pool. We'll have a real one by next summer. Right, Ry?

Alana couldn't blame Janie for wanting to be rescued from relentless weekend birthday parties and soccer games, punctuated by double time diaper changes, wispy hair encrusted with unknown substances, lost Band-Aids and mealy teething crackers lodged inside the leather seams of the Laughlin's Audi wagon.

Sounds like a plan, Alana said, turning back to the game. She imagined she might catch up with Janie and see Ryan in his habitat, all in one productive afternoon.

The coffee cart is here! Ryan, watch the girls! Janie ordered, as she marched through the gates of the rec center toward a cherry Danish. A family of five seemed tribal, an energetic pack of competing wants corraled by a maternal official.

As Janie sprinted toward the cart, Ryan turned to Alana. Man, I got back less than twenty-four hours ago and the house is like a battlefield house. The twins still wake up at night and Janie runs in and out. God knows how she sleeps. She's still nursing, but I guess that's her thing. Then Davis is so high energy at like six in the morning. Sometimes I feel like I'm just…in the way.

What do you mean? You're the dad.

Ryan smiled. Yeah, he said, hard to get back in after almost two months. Janie's got it all figured out.

Alana contemplated this sad confession while Ryan studied her.

Bangs. Is that what you did? He poked gently at her forehead.

I guess I needed a change, Alana said, remembering she'd cut her hair since she'd last seen him. It had already grown a bit.

You look good. With the sweatshirt and the bangs, you look like a kid.

Was it good to look like a kid? She felt exposed. Or maybe grateful to be seen.

Couples keep historical records, Alana thought. The history of us is repeated and revised, lost, and reimagined. After ten years of marriage, Alex knew the calibrations of Alana's day, the length and shape and vigor of her body, the rounding of her breasts in his palms, the enclaves of her anxious mind.

Today, at 41, she was all this and none of it: the hot middle-schooler with the Sassoon jeans, shag haircut, and fake I.D. who sipped a Tequila Sunrise from a tall glass and dragged on a Marlboro in a Greenwich Village bar at the age of 13; the irresponsible mother's helper who reluctantly mastered blow jobs in the dunes of Montauk, Long Island with Nick, her muscular, townie boyfriend; the New England college girl who majored in Women's Studies, slept with a visiting theatre director, while crushing on heroes like Didion, Sam Shepherd, Susan Sontag, Adrienne Rich, Patti Smith, Lou Reed, Scorsese, Bertolucci, and Goddard, and snorted too much blow with her incestuous housemates; the tortured playwright, fledgling journalist, and aspiring screenwriter, who escaped from New York to L.A., thinking she would give it six months to make some Hollywood connections; and now, the faithful wife and mother who struggled to hang on to a house they could not afford—only to exhale an anxious breath at the end of a young child's day.

I think that last goal just wrapped it up, Ryan said, folding up his chair. His tee shirt barely met the top of his shorts, and Alana noted that his wide, pale belly was larger than she had remembered. Maybe he drank a few too many beers or had a few too many helpings of the old craft services while in New York.

No matter. She could enjoy it. Marriage had taught her to accept, even delight, at times, in imperfections.

Alana felt the warmth of the sun on her freckled shoulder. In the brightness, Ryan's face was nearly erased, leaving only lashes and fleshy lips and a hint of the curved skateboarding scar above his lip that now read as a pale mustache.

The playing field was hazy now, filled with an indistinguishable mix of children's laughter and screams. Janie was heading back after stopping to chat with the other sporty families. Alana watched as Janie walked with Kayla against her chest, as if the child and mother were one organism once again.

I wish we could just leave all this and go for a cold beer, Ryan said.

All this was impossible to leave, Alana thought. Still she found herself wishing she could slip away coyly, without judgement, like the sun behind a cloud.

The temperature was arctic in Janie's house when Alana arrived later that afternoon. The older kids were still giddy outside, chasing each other with a garden hose. They showed no interest in ending what had been an exhausting day, held mostly in the patch of grass flanked by bougainvillea and an outdoor shower. Janie greeted the twins, who were locked into their matching high chairs like royalty. Each had made a chunky soup of applesauce with cinnamon topping.

They've been having a great time, Janie said. Clara beat Davis in ping-pong again and he gets this sulky attitude like his father. Clara just puts him in his place.

Alana was overwhelmed by all the new appliances and kitchen items, including a dazzling new espresso machine with Italian lettering, a blender she'd eyed in a catalog, and a set of colorful French cookwear stored on shelves or hung from a rack that doubled as the markings of modern success.

She pointed to a box on the counter. They found this in the garden. Davis wants to have a funeral and bury it later under the moonlight. Then he wants to have a séance. Care to join us?

Alana peered into the box. The bird was the size of a child's fist. Its head was fixed to its pale grey neck, and its body was lain out on a strip of white tissue paper, which curled at the ends, suggesting the ceremonial bed.

Janie opened up the Viking oven to a bubbling masterpiece of ground beef and spices, secured by a delicate layer of crusty dough. It sat inside its tinfoil tent like a well-appointed sheik.

Taste my meatless mousaka! It's outrageous, she said. I know it's hot outside, but I was in the mood.

Alana took a bite. Mmm. Incredible, she said.

Who even knows if Ryan's coming home for dinner, Janie said. I'm pissed at him.

Alana had shaved her legs in the shower, imaging he might take notice of her proud, shapely calves or her fresh pedicure, or some small detail about her as she whisked Clara out to the car.

Turns out he didn't have to make up one of the numerous parent-participation work days he'd missed at the school, said Janie. So he went out mountain-biking with his brother. He was home for a day and I guess he got fed up with us.

It's a bit hot for that, Alana said. I mean the mountain-biking—not the kids.

He's lost, Janie said, pouring herself a glass of wine. It's really sad.

She emerged from the pantry with a new bottle of expensive wine. Get this—he says he's *not sure* what's going on with this woman in New York.

Janie picked up the blue sippy cup Kayla had hurled from her high chair and placed it back on the tray. Cup stays on the tray, she said emphatically.

What—? Alana took it in.

Tee-nah. Some makeup artist-hunny who lives in Brooklyn.

Oh. You didn't mention...

Yeah, they're old buddies—apparently she works with this director a lot. She was on the movie in New York and Vancouver. He says it really has him confused about things.

Alana didn't know what there was to be confused about. It semed Ryan didn't love Janie anymore, at least not with passion. Couples suffering deaths of one kind or another seemed inescapable. Even the brightest stars eventually die. Some couples mourned these deaths, others tried to resurrect them, she thought, while others built walls of resentment.

Janie fed the twins and gave some scraps to Molly, the oversized Shepherd, who still barked ferociously at the postal workers dutifully arriving in their blue uniforms each day.

Ryan and I had this weird conversation last night, Janie said. Of course he was too tired to even— we haven't fucked in like a year.

Alana nodded, while Janie pulled Kayla and Maggie from their high chairs. He didn't really want—we didn't mean to have *twins*, you know. It was a surprise. A good surprise, but, I mean here we are.

Clara came running in to the kitchen in a damp halter-top and shorts with her hair soaking wet from being doused with a hose all afternoon.

Mom, can we go?

Sure, Sweetie. We'll go in five minutes, but I'm talking now. Go play with Davis.

He's cheating. You can't hit the ball twice. It's *one bounce* on each side. Will you tell him? Mah-ah-mm.

You tell him. Use your words. I'll be there in a minute. C'mon.

Clara's small body got swallowed up in the basement, as she yelled, one bounce!

Janie cleaned the twins' hands with a papery wipe. I could have been one of those *TV-writer-women*, she said, living in a big-ass house in Brentwood making a shit-ton of money.

Alana agreed. Janie could have been recognized and rich on her own. No doubt.

That couples suffered deaths of one kind or another seemed inevitable. Janie indicated a large belly with her hands. And he had this disappointed tone. *Why didn't you tell me you were the kind who wants to go to Mommy and Me?* The irony, of course, is that Ryan was the one from a big family who thought it was some kind of crime—child abuse—to have one kid—so, you know, we did the whole fertility thing.

I remember you said...

Needles in my stomach. Gearing up for sex like it was a perverse Olympic sport. Feet in the air... You know I even went to a shaman in Boyle Heights?

Alana was growing more uncomfortable thinking about all the effort made to breed, to create families, and the numerous ways in which people could fail to sustain them.

She does makeup? Alana wanted more answers about the girl.

It's pathetic, Janie said. Probably thinks Ryan's hot because he works with what's his name, Simon London. Wait 'til she's bending over to pick up Ryan's boxers off the floor.

How long has he been—how long?

I don't know that anything's *going on*, Janie corrected. He just talks about this *Tina-thing* each time he goes to New York, and this time when he talked about her, I could tell that something was wrong. You know your husband. You know the phony eyes, the things he repeats…his little obsessions.

Janie finished her wine and poured herself another glass.

I just looked at him and I told him, point blank, he's either in or he's out. I've worked too hard to make this whole thing work.

Really, Alana thought, swallowing one of the small and perfectly roasted peppers Janie had put in front of her.

I want to send her a message. Something like—I don't know—that dead bird Davis found on our back porch with its little broken neck.

Would you really do that?

Huh. You sound like you're on her side, Janie said, holding up her glass.

No, no, no, of course not.

It's hard to know what you would do, Janie said, until it happens to you. You can't hold someone down. You can't capture your partner in a net. But when they live in the greater world, there are those tempations. I guess.

Janie's face had changed. She looked resigned and sad, and a little flushed from the wine.

At that point, Clara, with paddle in hand, cried her way up the spiral stairs. The ping pong issue had escalated. Alana wrapped her in her arms. It was getting late. Time to leave the Laughlin house.

Six months ago, before Ryan left to shoot *Lazy Dreamers* in New York, they met up at a six-year-old's vegan birthday party, to which both Davis and Clara were invited. The kids were all sipping on their Capri juices, or kicking balls in the dusty park, or playing a ring toss game the host mom had arranged.

Ryan coplimented Alana on the dress she wore and asked if she wanted to go for a ride. Alana climbed on the motorcycle, saying good-bye to all that, as if she'd ended a past life with the wave of her hand.

They breezed through Griffith Park, leaning into the turns, averting potholes, and picking up speed like outlaws. Eventually, they picked a spot. Ryan killed the motor and placed his jacket down under a tree. There he cozied up to her, sitting dangerously close until his leg was touching hers, laughing like the old friends they were. He described the challenge of being on location for months at a time.

The rest of your life is on hold, Ryan explained. Doesn't matter who's waiting at home. It's kind of great but it's kind of awful, you know. To work so hard, but to be so loose, so unaccountable.

Alana tried to imagine trading in domestic routine for weeks on a set, but she had never had the right temperament for production. She'd bungled her job as a receptionist at a talent agency on Wilshire. They'd called her not *quick enough*. She'd been summarily fired from a stint as a producer's assistant for stuttering her way through a recap of his pink, *While You Were Out* phone messages. And her job with one of the town's biggest talent managers ended three weeks later with a dented Jaguar and an invite to dinner.

Believe me, Alana said, nothing's on hold while you're gone. We moms still carry on. You've only been spared the mundane.

His response was to light a cigarette. It's all good, Ryan said, sounding like a Californian. I guess I'm just one of the few who never mastered the matrix of family life. Those guys at the party, the dads back there, they figured out how to—I don't know—chase after the toddlers and keep everybody in new cars and whatever. Not me.

Alana thought it all sounded ominous for Janie and the kids. He was gone for months at a time. Soon he'd be on another project for several weeks, leaving his wife to entertain the troops in the modern house overlooking the reservoir.

She felt a buzz, a slightly spongy feeling as if things were softening as she finished her beer. Ryan sat closer to her, their shoulders touching.

Maybe it was then, under the tree, when she felt her younger self returning to her like a refrain from a favorite song, a song she'd lost but now remembered with great affection.

And when he reached for her under the tree and kissed her lips, she was surprised and ashamed—and somehow she was grateful. And she cherished that moment, thinking only of how free she felt in it. To be lost, and discovered, to be seen. To have, she thought, a change in status.

I'm sorry, he seemed to say, whispering into her hair.

She didn't know who exactly was at fault, so she didn't say anything at all.

On the ride back, she decided that the kiss was benign, nothing more than a fumble. But when she replayed it fast and slow, the kiss seemed to be years in the making. This was followed by the saddest moment of all: the revelation of what she had broken with Alex. Something had been snapped in two like a wishbone.

She and Ryan were the last parents to arrive for pick up.

Mama! Where were you? Clara called out.

Alana waved. Time to go, Bug, she announced too quietly for her daughter to hear.

Alana touched her lips, the lips that had been kissed.

The birthday boy's mom, a sporty-looking gal, picked up the oversized box that contained the remains of the cake and negotiated a spot for it in the van. Then, as Alana approached she turned to greet her with a frown.

Hey there, Clara's mom? I called your cell a few times. Did you go on vacation?

As she spoke, Alana noticed a trace of pink frosting, smeared like lipstick, across her upper lip.

Alana could see Clara running toward her down the path with a goodie bag in her hand. Clara's smile was joyful, her eyes bright and fixed only on her mother's face.

Do you think Ryan's having an affair? Alana asked over breakfast.

Alex raised his brows and yawned. I don't know. Is he?

There's some girl in New York, Janie says. *Tina?*

Alex smiled. Ryan's been out of town for a good part of the year. He does his thing… and Janie does hers, along with three kids. I mean, right?

Alana popped the bread in the toaster. Do you know anything?

Like what? Alex opened and shut the fridge.

Like anything? Alana asked.

Not really.

Not really? Does that mean yes, but you don't want to tell me?

It's not even nine in the morning and you're interrogating me about your boyfriend? You should know if he's fucking around.

My what?

Alex grinned. He had been paying attention. C'mon, Ryan's always been your little fantasy boy. His perfect hair and his multiple pairs of kicks. I love the guy, but we all know he's vain as shit.

Janie thinks he's been with some makeup girl in New York.

Really? Is she cute?

Seriously, Alana said. Janie's had it.

Alex sounded rational.

He's on location and she's home. You know that kind of shit happens a lot in this town.

So, Alana said, I should be glad we spend every waking minute of the day bobbing around the ocean together like plankton?

Maybe you should appreciate that you have a husband who puts up with your daily neuroses, and your nightly anxiety.

Trust me, you should be very anxious—but you're too stoned.

Thank God for weed.

Alana continued. We could get a lot of money for this house—before they take it away from us.

Alex batted smoke away from the toaster and rescued a piece of toast. Alex sat down at the kitchen table to butter it.

Can I just have my coffee, please? In peace.

You know we could double—maybe even triple—what we paid for this place, Alana said. The people down the block...

Alex raised his voice. I don't give a shit about the people down the block.

You know what, hoping and crossing your fingers and packing a morning bowl to face the day just isn't enough. You've got to do something, Alana said.

This is me doing *something*. I'm drinking my fucking coffee.

Yeah, no.

I can't drink my coffee, Alana?

We can't pay our bills. We have one shitty car from another decade that's on its last legs, and another one that's unregistered and has no brakes.

We're going to take care of it.

Alex got up from the table and stood with his back to her, fiddling with the toaster.

But you're not, she said. You're not taking care of it. I'm bouncing checks, Alana went on. I'm starting to dodge people. I avoid seeing people we know in the aisles at TJ's because we owe them money.

Things are going to get better.

When?

I'll sell a painting. There's a guy from a Brooklyn gallery...

Yeah.

Just fucking stop, Alana. Stop your complaining and live with your disappointment—this is what you've got. Real life. This is it.

Alex slipped out to the yard, slamming the screen door for effect.

Alana retreated to the bedroom where she conjured a long-range view of life-without-Alex: the inglorious 12-hour-a-day job she would take at the PR agency, promoting high end hair gel and designer sweatpants, the solemn breakfasts, the redecoration of the new rental—where? In an up and coming Glassell Park? Alhambra? Her visits to the meditation center in Frogtown where she might return to her dharma and meet someone who was—what? *More present? More in the moment?* And keep what she would miss about Alex: his quirky jokes supported by a hearty laugh, his unwavering optimism, his navigational skills, his standing on a ladder to reach a corner of the canvas, or the way he spread the paint on the canvas like batter. She would miss what they once had in bed. She would ache for the smooth expanse and hardness of his body, the blue veins and dark flesh, the elegant fingers, the calming effect he had on her mind.

She imagined herself struggling to stay afloat during Clara's turbulent teenage years, as Clara planned her devious escape to adulthood and Alex, finally recognized here and abroad for his works on paper, launched his solo career in her absence.

Should she take the soul-crushing job at the agency downtown?

She'd have stability: a 401k or something that steadily matured as she did. And, if she never encountered that pragmatic, Heal-the-Bay, Sub-uru-driving ambitious Husband Number II at the Vermont Canyon tennis courts… or at a Michel-torena barbecue… or a school recital at which public defender dads lamented the mounting class sizes in LAUSD (35 kids is five too many!), she might just live out her greying years in a pool-centered com-munity. Maybe she'd find something nice on Los Feliz Boulevard—dream on.

She thought Alex might consider trading up to some young Cal Arts hottie with a city pension, re-liable breasts, and a bobbed hairdo who arrived on her vintage Raleigh bike to a group show at a Culver City gallery. Alana might run into Alex with his sinewy lady friend at New Spanish Cinema at The Cinemathéque. They'd have a nostalgic exchange about their early '90s trip to Spain when Alana wrote for the travel mag, and they got comped in the honeymoon suites of the *paradores*.

When Alana was done with her septic ruminations about the future, she peeked out the window and caught a glimpse of her husband pacing in his studio. She stood at the doorway, watching him work. There was something compelling about the way he hovered in front of the canvas, engaged in a silent conversation. He dabbed at the edges, dipped the brush in the mix of blue paint, and tilted his head to view the scene from a new angle. Although he had always invited her to watch him work and welcomed her candid critiques, today she felt voyeuristic.

Does this work? He would ask referring to a section that suggested a disembodied form. I can't get the sky quite right.

It works, yeah. Maybe take this line away and that looks more like the sea stops there and the sky begins.

The conversation about his work was a constant. For more than a decade, he had painted for himself and looked to her for impressions. In turn, she wrote new scenes or feature stories and asked him to read early drafts. That hadn't changed over the years. Art partners forever.

Days like today, Alejandro Amaro seemed no different from the guy she had met at the screen-writer's party in the canyon all those years ago. She had first seen him poolside: the boy with the glasses held together by gaffer's tape, and a striped Brooks Brothers shirt splattered with paint. The *rebel* tamed by East Coast schools, the self-contained semiotician, determined to grow weed among the potted cacti on a Venice rooftop, drink his heart-thumping espressos and make art.

Alana walked closer to his painting. The scene suggested trees, cryptic symbols under a surreal sky layered in hues of purple grey.

This series is beautiful, she said. I told you that the other night, but you weren't listening.

Alana liked the familiar smell of oil paint and the hint of turpentine. She liked the dusty sketch-books and stacks of Polaroid photos, and the sloping wood beams of the studio ceiling. She liked the coffee stains in concentric rings on the big oak table, the window garden filled with budding succulents in coffee cans and mismatched pots.

One day, she hoped, they'd have the money to fix the studio before the roof caved in. This moment was like so many other quiet moments spent in the studio with Alex. Yes, there were losses. Yes, there were gains. For now, they remained.

Wordlessly, Alana asked her husband for a kiss.

Alex pressed his lips to her cheek, then her mouth, and pulled her close.

They were surrounded by Alex's paintings, a parade of enigmatic glyphs, and somber images. Alana could feel an eager breeze on her shoulders, as she and Alex stood perfectly still, kissing like sculptures. They had crossed a divide, they had spoken less than all the truth, they had contemplated how they might continue, how they might creep along, limp along, or thrive. How they might thrive in the absence of one another.

For All You've Done

Palm Springs, 2008

From the neck up Alana's father is as she would like to remember him, the swarthy guy, the funny guy, the irrepressible guy, the lion in the living room. The guy who once played a mean game of tennis with his retail cronies at the courts in Queens. She remembers the days of his crisp white polo shirts and shorts, dancing up to the net on stocky, muscular legs. She remembers his cool terrycloth wristbands, Rod Laver sneakers, the cream-colored, cable-knit tennis sweaters, the big-faced Prince racket, and the pock! sound that the ball made against it. She remembers the stash of sugar cubes, each one a piece of white gold, zipped inside the vinyl cover— just in case.

Now Stan inhabits a failed body. He carries a stomach bloated by a mystery fluid that festers inside him in a hardening mass. His left leg is missing. In its place is a sad, stumpy thing with an ace bandage at the tip, no kneecap.

Alana remembers his leg fondly. Her father's leg. And she wonders why it had to die before the rest of him. Peeking out from under the sheet, she sees his good leg, the one that could support him if it had to. On it rests one of his weary testicles, which has grown to the size of a grapefruit.

Did you get the paper, Al? Stan sounds desperate. Your mother forgets to bring it in every time.

Alana hands him the sports section, leaving the front page and Calendar at the foot of the bed.

Sometimes I think if her head wasn't screwed on to her body—. Stan purses his mouth and makes a popping sound. It's a dry kiss made by dry lips, but she'll take it. She hands him his glasses, knowing that he's going blind, and stares off into space.

In the newly remodeled kitchen of Stan's house there are childhood pictures of Alana. She is waving from atop her bike in Central Park. Holding up a trophy at Lake Placid summer camp. She's looking both awkward and sultry as teen, posed in front of the Christmas tree in a black velvet dress. Beside the teen photo is a wedding picture taken on a California lawn: Alana and Alex, young and full of promise, feeding each other cake. Below the clock, a series of Clara, the only grandchild, small and exhausted from a game of Pee Wee soccer.

The kitchen is where Alana's mother, June, makes her tarts, her sweet desert crepes, and her lemony chicken. It's where she smokes her low tars, does her crosswords, and reads her recipes. It's where June talks of Stan in quiet tones that won't disturb the sick, in more of a hush than a whisper: the surgeon couldn't believe an 81-year-old diabetic still had a head of hair like that... too weak for dialysis...last time he could really walk was the summer before we sold the New York apartment...he likes it when you read to him, something upbeat—nothing heavy...David Sedaris...Emily Dickinson.

When June bends down, Alana sees that her jeans are too roomy; she has lost 15 pounds worrying about Stan. Alana imagines that her mother is as thin as she was when she kicked her sculpted legs in musicals and reviews, or when she modeled for Picone on Seventh Avenue. Even with worry imbedded in her face, June has always had a reserve tank of beauty; she's still the kind of woman who elicits a gasp when her age is revealed.

He likes the canned soups better than my lentils, June whispers, holding on to Alana's arm like she did when she taught her how to cross the intersection at 96th and Broadway. You know your father, if he doesn't like the food, he's a royal pain in the ass.

June says she may lie down when Gus comes for his shift at two o'clock. Alana says, *you do that*, remembering how much June loves her naps in the wicker day-bed on the porch—her only escape now that things like dry vermouth and Librium are no longer on the menu.

Gus's old jeep rumbles along, hitting the gravel driveway with a hiss. Alana watches through the rectangular window in the living room as he gets out of his car, drags hard and deep on a Camel, and steps it out with his sneaker. Alana wishes she could smoke, but she's been trying—again—for weeks to quit. She feels a stirring when Gus arrives, relieved to have another witness, an ally in the room.

Gus is compact and cheerful, bad teeth, muscular arms toasted by the desert sun, scruff around his chin, and has thick black hair nearly to his shoulders. He is Stan's caretaker, his friend and paid companion. The one who helps June with all the mess. He cleans bedpans, changes sheets, picks up Stan's insulin supplies at the Sav-On, and entertains Stan with stories of his youthful escapades.

Gus starts his shift by opening the blinds. The sun frames the bedroom in a widening coat of afternoon light, and Stan pushes up in his bed to greet it. Gus puts on his uniform, a white lab coat, and slips a pair of clear elastic gloves on his hands. He smiles at Alana, calling her Alana de la Garza, a TV actress he likes.

Stan lifts his arm, and Gus dabs it with an alcohol-soaked cotton ball before piercing him with the shot he needs for the afternoon. Stan doesn't wince; he breathes out and takes in the view. Flat stretches for miles, green appearing only as an accent in the brush, and wrinkly mountains shoved up against the sky. He's used to urban scenes: brick, pre-war buildings, concrete and glass, smooth sidewalks that glitter in the warmer months, man-made islands with a few well-placed plants separating the traffic. But this one—the cactus, the pebbles, the palm trees, the warm turquoise swimming pools and sandy lawns—works well enough for his final days.

Stan reminds Gus that Alana is a writer, that she's just finished an article for a magazine.

You interviewed—who was it—De Niro?

Yeah. He won an award, Dad.

She's done a few of those, he tells Gus. Then he turns to Alana and asks, Any kind of pay?

Alana doesn't answer. She's preoccupied with the foreclosure notice from the mortgage company that waits on her desk, the overgrown grass on the front lawn, the busted taillight on the aging car, the feeling that things are not okay at home. She's worried about her untreated puffy gums, her somber facial expressions, the darkening mole on her back, her busy mind. She's anxious about Clara's book report, and her daughter's weekly headaches. She's worried about Clara's uneaten lunches, her nightmare about a burning house, her waking in the middle of the night. She's conflicted about Alex, his lack of work, his paralytic state, his dwindling bag of weed sprouting from his bedside table, his glacial responses, his entitlement issues, his rebellious spirit that seems to run contrary to what Stan taught her about taking care of things.

Stan seems determined to keep up with the world outside his bed. He reminds Alana that, despite her ambivalence, she married the real thing. Alex is really an artist, Stan says artists don't go straight, they don't wake up and change. He warns her that it's not prudent to push anything. Artists won't go to regular jobs, he says—at least not without dying a little. He suggests that she be the one to keep things stable, maybe get a real job—marketing or something for a while, for however long. Then Stan makes his simple demands.

I want to see my girl, my granddaughter. It's time for them to get in the car—did you get it fixed?—and come to Palm Springs.

Alana nods, and assures him they'll be here tomorrow.

The doctors say I'm filling up with fluid. Kidneys are shot, he says. If you ain't got kidneys, you ain't got nothin'. Tell your artist-husband not to miss the main event.

As Gus's shift is ending Stan tells Gus about Alana's latest plan, tells him that Alana is no longer drifting. First it was Women's Studies—what the hell you going to do with that degree? Stan asks rhetorically.

Then it was the crazy ashram upstate. He tells him that she's thinking about teaching, that she's good with kids. Alana's reassured to hear her father's version of who she is, or who she might become. In this rare moment, he doesn't put her down, and she doesn't offer up her losses.

Alana doesn't say how she wishes she could have done it right, sold the script for six figures, married the right guy for Stan, become a noted *someone* in the world of *something*. She doesn't say what she told her shrink about how, at 43, she wishes she could add up to more, be more of a presence, have more of Stan's greatness embedded in her DNA.

She thinks about the typewriter Stan gave her with the onionskin paper curled inside:

> *Dearest Al,*
>> *This machine may be a conduit*
>> *For all your fertile thoughts –*
>> *or at least the ones that beg to be re-*
> *corded.*
>> *All my love,*
>> *Dad*
>> *Christmas, 1982*

Shaven and patted down with a towel, Stan leans back

against the pillow with his arms outstretched. He calls for June. Joo-ooon.

He wants his pajamas.

My wife whisked them away and put them in the goddamn dryer two hours ago and then—poof—no sign of her, Stan says. That woman has disappeared off the face of the Earth.

Alana weakly defends her mother. She says you're refusing to wear them.

Stan thinks that's crap. Would you please get them for me before I shiver to death?

Stan motions to a stack of CDs. On a day like this, let's hear some Sinatra, he says.

Gus pushes the button on the CD player.

...It was just one of those things
Just one of those crazy flings...

Stan sings along for a minute—*a trip to the moon on gossamer wings*—before his eyelids drop mast, and he drifts off. Gus lowers the volume until the words are barely there, and leans over Stan, watching him breathe. He puts up the bar on the bed, tucks in the corners of the sheets. Then he reaches for Alana's hand.

Pray with me a minute, he says, so quietly it's barely audible.

She resists, not one for real prayer, not sure how.

But Gus's face looks serene, like a handsome

young saint, like a Sinatra convert, like the only one in the room who knows what might come next. Alana closes her eyes, bows her head and takes Gus's hand. Her silent prayer feels weak, decaffeinated. She tries to think of something hopeful. Seeing her father at the end of his life, pretending that these are not a series of final conversations, feels more impossible than anything else.

Alana sits on a bench next to Gus in the backyard. He tells her she looks hot in her dark colored blouse. He says he wears white to keep off the heat and to look professional. She stares down at the modernist pavers that have turned a worldly grey, the color of storm clouds and old men's whiskers.

Gus offers her a cigarette. She tells him, tells herself she's quit—but she'll just have a drag.

How much time do you think he has? Alana asks, staring straight ahead.

Gus shrugs. Your dad, he's a tough guy. Hard to say.

My dad and I were talking and we want you to have the car, you know, Stan's old Saab when—later on, Alana says.

Gus stands up and shakes his head. I couldn't—.

No, really, Alana says. We want you to have it. Stan wants you to have it. He said you know how to drive it. My mother can't really drive a stick shift. It's yours, okay? For all you've done.

I don't know, Gus says. He seems to be holding back a grin.

Well, I do, Alana says. You'll look good driving around in that car. Does your wife drive?

Oh, yeah. Bus driver for schools over in Indio/ Palm Desert area where we live. Out of the house at 5:30 every morning.

Alana thinks about Gus and his wife waking before dawn and dressing in silence. Thinks about his driving to work in the Saab, top down, radio pumping something cool. Then she remembers that Gus won't come to work at Stan's house. And her father won't live at that house anymore. Stan won't live at the Palm Springs house where he was planning to retire but never did. He'll be somewhere else. She's not sure where. Heaven is too convenient. Out in the ether seems too vague. He won't be part of a well-tended lawn some-where; that's not his style.

They decide to take the Saab for a spin and to get some supplies. They head out towards town, then decide on a detour near the municipal courts and head down North Palm Canyon Drive.

This thing hugs the road, Gus says. Europeans, they make good cars.

Gus slows in the late afternoon traffic, adjusting the radio with a tap.

Pull over, there's a turn-out up there, says Alana. Amazing view.

Gus slips out of the traffic and turns off the road. A mountainside hovers above them. The car slows near a long dirt canyon that leads to a waterfall. Beds of succulents and spiky plants that look like they were grown on another planet. Shady sections filled with patches of thick, ocher brush.

You got a divorce? Gus kills the engine and stares straight ahead.

No, no divorce, says Alana. Why? Stan probably told you we have problems. He's worried, I guess.

She figures Gus has heard it all from Stan. He'll accept her partial response.

Gus stops the car by the side of the road. He opens the back door, lays his denim jacket down in the back seat and pulls Alana onto his lap. As he unbuttons her shirt, his face is serious, purposeful. He moves his hands and lips across the crescent shape of her breasts. He grins, as he tastes her creamy skin. He touches her with hands that have cared for the injured, careful hands that have plucked splinters from children's feet, pulled hooks from the mouths of fish, held the weight of a saxophone, and wrestled in sand and dirt with six brothers.

A stranger's hands.

Gus lifts her skirt, slides his hands across her thighs. Alana struggles to open his heavy silver buckle, wads his shirt in a ball. He smells like lemony cologne mixed with his sweat and something antiseptic. She runs her tongue across the crack in his tooth. Salve to a wound. Gus whispers, holding her head as she gets him hard. *Jesus. Jesus.*

What is it she feels? She's suspended some-where, her body as light as string, the night drifting down from the rounded edges of the hillside. She is all tongue, all moist, all touch, all flavor, all flesh, all gone.

The house is quiet, undisturbed when she returns. No warning but the quiet sound of June's exhalations, June's sorrow.

Nothing could have prepared Alana for the vision of her mother, crouched at the side of the bed, her two fingers, stroking Stan's left hand. And there was nothing Alana had ever seen that compared to the surreal notion of Stan, a leathery version that was cold and still.

By the time Alana arrived, all the warmth that made him a lion had seeped out. Nothing left in place but skin and hair, eyelids that June had drawn shut with her fingertips. Dry lips that would never make the pop-ping sound for a kiss. A stiffened leg. A missing one.

June motioned for Alana to come closer. Her face was distorted as she whispered. He said something to me just an hour ago, just before—he said, You and me, June, we've been close for a very long time.

As a child, Alana had seen her mother unsure of Stan's love, making accusations, behaving badly, curled in a ball, slurring her speech at lunchtime, forgetting her keys, burning dinners, imagining his infidelity while abroad, threatening again and again to leave him. But now she sees where June has landed, sees her at the foot of Stan's bed. She sees June looking for signs of the guy she first met on the Fire Island ferry in '59. The funny guy, the once virile guy, the tennis playing retail king from the Upper West Side. The guy who said New York was over, and promised sunny days in California, closer to the grandchild, a place to thrive, not a good place to shrivel up and die. The lion in the living room.

Where did you go? June asks, her head against the pillow. We've got to phone everyone. Let everybody know.

The memorial for Stan is held at his brother's modernist house at the top of a Canyon. Alana and June sit side by side on the flowered sofa like droopy dolls in their loose black dresses, fingers laced together, sharing a

Coke. Later everyone gathers and they listen to speeches from Stan's retail friends, from his platoon and college buddies. They hear about Stan's youthful pranks, about his Foxtrot, his Lindy style, about his muttonchops and his war protests, his art and rare book collections, and his yen for shortwave radios, bikes and vintage cars. They talk about his early days as high school valedictorian at DeWitt Clinton, his airborne war years, his insomnia, his workaholism, his Montblanc pens, Saville Row suits and fine leather jot pads, his dirty jokes, and his disgust for mayonnaise on deli sandwiches. The family friends from New York—the well-heeled elders dressed formally against the dry Palm Springs weather—speak slowly about Stan, calling him, *the worst driver you ever knew*, *a helluva salesman*, *a cunning doubles player*, *a ladies' man*. Over Frank Sinatra, they talk about the early days, Stan's move to Peter Cooper with his first, post-war wife. They praise the gorgeous June, *a star of stage and runway, a dedicated wife, an around-the-clock nurse, and one terrific gal*.

In between the speeches, Alana goes outside for a smoke. She's hoping Alex and Clara will arrive any minute. She's hoping he'll arrive and hold her while all the guilt, all the suffering, all the sadness empties out. A jeep comes up the long gravel driveway and Gus emerges, groomed and wearing a dark jacket, white shirt, and pressed slacks. Alana feels a wave of regret for things left unsaid—or for indulgence, she's not sure—but it is quickly eclipsed by the weight of her loss.

Gus looks at Alana, swallows, and looks down at his shoes. Sorry about your *papi*.

Alana hugs him, her lips close to the veins in his neck.

Lot of people here, he says, pointing to the crowd inside.

Alana nods. You coming in?

He hesitates and says, I have to talk to you for a minute. I've got a problem. Something bad happened. There was an accident yesterday and I don't have your father's car no more.

What?

This other car… over there on Tahquitz Canyon… my wife broke a few bones in her hand and she has her ribs all bruised up. The girls and me just got whiplash, thank God. But the car. It's messed up. It's completely—

I'm so sorry, Alana says. That's—but you're okay? The girls are okay?

Yeah, thank God, we're good. We're doing okay. Gus holds up his bandaged wrist.

Listen, he continues, I know you're busy, but I

got to ask you this…damn…forget it.

What, Gus? C'mon.

It's the medical bills. They're wiping us out, you know. Like $5,000 and I didn't have no insurance on the car.

Alana responds, That's awful. I'm so sorry to hear that.

She pauses. I've got to get back inside. Come in and have some food. We can talk about this later. Not now.

You said you wanted to help us, right?

Yeah, but, I mean—

Can you just write us a check? Then go back to the party.

It's not a party, Gus. Jesus Christ.

Gus looks menacing. You don't get it, do you? You want to make me beg? You want to humiliate me some more, don't you?

June pokes her head out of the door and motions for Alana.

Gus turns his back to June. Alana waves *I'll be right there*.

June raises her eyebrows and disappears inside.

It's not my fault. It was an accident, Gus insists.

Help us out. C'mon, a thousand bucks. I know

you've got it.

You want me to give you a thousand—? Now? Are you crazy?

Gus's eyes bulge. Okay, okay. What have you got? Five hundred?

This is a memorial, Alana turns away.

You owe me, Gus says, like a threat.

My father is dead.

But you said you'd help us, Gus pleads.

You need to leave—Now.

Cheap Jews Gus says, under his breath.

Alana grabs his shirt. Get out.

Gus motions to a friend in the driver's seat of his old jeep. The car pulls up and Gus jumps in. Alana watches as they drive over a flowerbed, murdering some newly planted azaleas, and fly through the gate, past the flat top hedges, down the driveway and into the seething desert night.

Inside the house, she blends into the mass of dark suits and dresses swarming the buffet table. Heads bobbing. Faces melting, small cousins in velvety skirts eating cold cuts and powdery desserts. Sinatra crooning in the background.

She feels unbalanced, like she might be ill. In the downstairs bathroom, she throws water on her face, wipes her mouth with the embroidered hand towel. She remembers a night like this from years ago at her uncle's house. A birthday was it? Stan at the piano, one leg pressing on the pedals. June over his shoulder, her hair pinned up in a hive, a touch of Chanel No. 5 behind her ears.

Alana hears her father's voice above all the rest. He sounds tired from all the deals made on the phone, all the traveling overseas, all the telling of the real and exaggerated stories that only he could tell. His voice is deep and firm, an imprint as unmistakable as her own skin.

A Condo in Redondo
Los Angeles, 2009

Pia Kovic sped down the hallway toward her third period English class, her heavy bag filled with papers slung across her shoulder. She could feel a student was gaining on her, but she refused to be derailed. As she turned the corner, she heard a familiar voice: I need a C or better on that essay, Ms. Kovic, he said. If I don't pass, I have to repeat. And I can't repeat. Please tell me you came through.

Ruben knew the art of the doorway ambush, with his big smile and noisy skate shoes that squeaked as he dashed across the linoleum floors. Kovic faltered slightly, clutching her bag to her chest.

Whatever you earned is what you got, my friend, Kovic said, remembering his essay about the American Dream as being thoughtful, despite the numerous run-ons.

...even if your not born with good circumstances or you make some mistakes you can push hard and never give up to get a good opportunity for your family...

Actually, you did pretty well, Ruben, she assured him. You weren't here last week when I gave the papers back. You passed, okay?

Oh, shit, I mean, thank you, Ruben said, trailing her to her desk. He then got close enough for Kovic to smell his young man's body, and while it wasn't a bad smell, it didn't feel right to get a whiff.

When I was writing the essay, I realized something.

That you should use transitions? Kovic said, unpacking a ringed notebook.

Nah, I was thinking you remind me of what we're reading. You're like Daisy in the book. You know that?

Miss Kovic shifted her weight and put her hair behind her ears, like a girl who'd been asked to the prom.

For real, he said. You're like Gatsby.

What? I thought I was like Daisy. She smiled.

You know, you're like classical, he said.

In refuge behind her desk, she balanced herself on the hard wooden chair.

Look, Ruben. You have to come to class, okay? No more absences. Good thing you turned in your essay, but I can't pass you if you don't show up.

Ruben turned up his lip in a kind of snarl. I've got a lot going on, you know.

Believe me, I've got a lot going on, too, Kovic said.

Yeah, Ruben nodded. I got a kid. A little girl, Sofia. She's really something, I'm telling you.

Kovic looked surprised. The baby's mom is at Marshall?

Nah, you don't know her. She tried high school for a while, but she's home now. Baby needs her all the time, so Carolina can't do anything else while her mom's at her job. She's trying to get her tia to come from El Salvador to help out.

Kovic imagined Ruben with a pacifier in between his big knuckles, cooing to his little one in the back seat as he cruised down Virgil, back to his neighborhood. Back to his life of hard-working parents, youthful grandparents, and kids having kids. She thought it must be a life that loomed much larger and pulled harder than his class in English Lit.

The third period bell sounded, and a few kids arrived, taking seats in the back row. That's when Ruben leaned over the teacher's desk and spoke quietly.

So, you got a man, Ms. Kovic?

Kovic felt herself freeze up. I don't know if

that's something I want to talk about, Ruben. We're about to get started. Why don't you take a seat.

So, nobody then? He asked again.

She grinned. I didn't say that. Ruben, take a seat.

That evening the sun had disappeared early as it did in the winter months, making the days seem to end without warning. At home, while heating up the leftovers for herself, she was bothered by Ruben's simple question. She had been dating Gordon Schneider, an entertainment lawyer, for more than a year, and the time had come to decide. Something.

Gordon was regular, if pedigreed; nothing aberrant or quirky about him. He was from a long line of USC-bred attorneys who prided themselves on sensibility and restraint. The kind of man who budgeted, calculated, and revised. He had grown up in South Pas, spent some vacations in Hawaii, or surfing in Orange County with his cousins. He thought of himself as a liberal; he'd voted for Obama and was grateful not to know too much about suffering. He made generous contributions to refugee causes, disease prevention, and bought chocolate bars outside the supermarket. All that checked out just fine.

He wasn't anything like the guys she'd met online and occasionally resurrected when feeling particularly lonely. Not like the 'shroom-eating wedding photographer obsessed with black and while images of ankles, earlobes, and toes. Or even like lovely Anick, the high school French teacher who seduced her over wine and cheese after a film club meeting at her Elysian Park home. He was high-functioning and athletic Gordon Schneider. Funny on occasion, especially when you got him doing an imitation of Arnold Schwarzenegger groping women in an elevator. And Gordon was married.

Each weekday morning, Gordon left his Spanish revival in Hancock Park, pecked Diane's temple, and went to work in his energy-efficient Prius, a conscious choice that supplanted the Beemer he'd had in the previous decade.

At the firm, he worked long hours and was marked quicky as a rising star who pleased clients and CFOs with his penchant for making deals that paid out plentifully over time. Points. Masterful addendums and clauses. Ancillary rights. Residuals up the wazoo. At night, he relaxed with a beer or a Stoli on the rocks, while ordering tickets, making reservations, or watching sports on TV.

On their first date, Gordon took Pia to Disney Hall as part of the world music series he'd subscribed to. As a female drum soloist from Scotland performed a rousing number in her bare feet, Kovic spied the ring on Gordon's left hand and felt a sharp pain. An elbow to the stomach. He hadn't mentioned that he had a wife when they were giddily exchanging numbers, or when talking earnestly about the problems with L.A.'s public school system. Or even when Kovic mentioned that she wasn't sure that she wanted a family, since she already had so many kids. When she gently confronted him about his wife after the concert, Gordon smiled like a boy caught stealing change from his mother's purse.

I should have said something, he admitted, sucking the last bit of ice from his drink. But we were having such a nice time, and I didn't want to kill the mood.

Kovic felt a general sense of ease with Gordon, a belief that all her hours doing difficult work were rewarded somehow by the amenities he provided. In Kovic's Protestant family there was a tacit agreement that life's frills were limited; work was our real purpose. They knew there was sorrow and grief breathing around every corner, but still believed we owed it to the world to work overtime. They frowned on adultery, despite the fact that Kovic's father had lovers who frequented the sign shop he ran in their Central Valley town. She didn't think her father would have approved of Gordon. He'd have said he put on airs.

Her father said Californians only needed two ties, one for a wedding and one for a funeral.

Frustrated during a spell of guilt about Gordon's marital status, Kovic had used her inner warrior to break it off a couple of times. Don't call me for a while, she'd say. I have a lot of papers to grade.

Most recently, on New Year's Eve, when she found herself alone in her apartment with her overweight cat Hermione, she waited to see if Gordon would remember to check on her. When he did, it was from a former frat buddy's party in the Palisades with Diane in the next room. Kovic couldn't bear to hear the reverie in his voice as he pretended he was calling his neurotic sister, a paralegal who he said complained of imagined allergies and had voted for Mitt Romney.

You're so right, sis, he slurred into the phone, it's better not to leave your house on New Year's. Too many checkpoints, drunk dudes, and gunshots.

That did it. Kovic was no longer willing to be kept on ice. Enough with the cryogenics. She swore she would move on to someone more available when the school year ended. She'd find someone who had the ping pongs to tell his wife it was done.

When they reconciled, Gordon brought a decent bottle of Spanish wine from the shop in the mini-mall. He drank a glass and got loose with his affection. He said he missed Pia terribly and that he had been doing a lot of thinking.

Kovic had felt confused, maybe even relieved by his absence. She took a moment and started her interrogative: I guess you're in love again, aren't you?

What do you mean again? Gordon said.

I hear that happens with people who are married a long time. They think it's dead in the water, a commuter train derailed. And then—boom!—they get it back. Start screwing like banshees!

Banshees, huh, Gordon said. That's a new one. She's the same old Diane. If she were a mattress, she'd be a reliable, firm Posturepedic, I guess.

Wow, Kovic said, the same old Diane who's fluent in Russian and Hebrew

—and French and English, Gordon added.

The Diane who can turn herself into a donut in yoga class, Kovic said.

A pretzel, Gordon corrected.

A what?

A pretzel, not a donut. Never mind.

And you're probably still convinced she'd

'go Unabomber'—if you were to tell her that you've found someone who's more like you, someone who likes nature documentaries, hiking, and a broad range of sushi. A woman who's…alive.

Telling her all that at this point would be a very poor idea, Gordon said, rifling through the kitchen drawers. Where are the takeout menus? Here's an idea—ding!—keep them all in one place.

Oh, fuck you, Gordon, she said.

Hey, no, don't say that to me.

No, I'm not taking it back. I'm not going to un-fuck my fuck you.

Pia, where did that come from?

Kovic looked at the clock in the kitchen and felt her stomach growl. It came from me, Gordon. I'm tired of your put-downs.

Well then, Gordon said. A gummy smile spread across his face.

Kovic paused, unsure what came next.

Nothing to see here, Gordon. We're two people who never should have met at that stupid barbeque. You're not, you're just not…available.

Okay, okay, let's not—I'm here, aren't I? Look at me. I'm here!

But she's there. She got there first, Kovic said. She's already living with you, doing laps in the pool.

93

That's what you negotiate at work, isn't it, ownership rights? Otherwise, we'd probably be living together by now, you know? I mean, can't we be realistic about…we have this and she has that. It's up to you to just finish her off.

Gordon looked a bit stunned, like he shouldn't laugh. Or maybe he should.

Finish her off?

Kovic handed him the take-out menu.

I'll have the vegetable moo-shu, she said.

Ruben was on the clock. He had to make it to each address on the list and get the van back before closing. He figured it was hard, but better than a lot of jobs. Better than his father's short order shifts at Manny's on Figueroa, better than the one his mother had sewing arms on nightgowns in that factory until she got the headaches. Better than his little brother Osito selling weed at the middle school, and maybe better than what his cousin Jonny would find in Iraq. He had responsibilities to a little girl and her mami. Finishing high school no longer seemed important. That was something you did if you had parents who pushed it. Or if you couldn't make bank.

About a month or two passed when his boss said he had another offer. He would teach Ruben to do home installations of flat screen TVs. Better money, he explained. Better neighborhoods. A skill. Ruben was grateful for that. He learned quickly and didn't question how Mike got into this after-hours business. He didn't ask why the deliveries flew from one loading dock to another with nods and hand-shakes and missing paper trails. Or why Mike was always loaded up with stacks of cash.

At the end of the month, when he held his little Sofia in his arms, and gave Carolina an envelope with six bills, he thanked Mike for hooking him up. Then he thanked God for his on-the-side job that was fast becoming his way of life.

One afternoon around five, Ruben drove by Carolina's and saw her sitting on the steps of her building with Sofia, his baby girl. They looked like they were having fun, like two sisters instead of mother and daughter, laughing together on the steps.

She doesn't want to crawl anymore, Carolina said. She holds on to things to pull herself up.

Crawling's overrated, Ruben joked. Then he twirled Sofia around, shading his face from the sun with her diaper padded butt. Look, she's flying. *Zooom.*

You growing a beard, or what? Carolina asked.

She leaned her head back, running her tiny hands through her long stretch of hair. She wasn't pretty like Ruben's mother or strong like his abi. Instead, Carolina had a cute bunny's face with large eyes, and a few faint scars above her eyebrows from when her brother pushed her out of a tree. Her lips stayed separated, making room for her upper teeth which pushed out slightly.

Ruben thought about when he first talked to Carolina at the lunch table in middle school. She was shy and kind of churchy, not the kind of girl he usually liked. Now, they sat on the steps with their child, talking like old friends.

You still go to school sometimes? Carolina asked.

Not too much lately, Ruben said. Too busy. You still thinking about getting your equivalent?

Who knows, Carolina said. Can't even think about that right now. I mostly miss my friends.

I know you got the baby, but don't give up on yourself, okay?

Carolina shrugged, bouncing Sofia in her lap. I might do hairstyling with my cousin. So.

Well, Ruben said, we could get married if you want.

Married, she repeated, with a funny look in her eyes.

She found a stretchy and put Sofia's hair in a ponytail. I love her so much it hurts me, you know. It gets me like I'm sick or something. I'm telling you. It's so weird.

It's not weird, Ruben said. That's normal.

He looked at Carolina, the youngest mami in the world, with her flowing hair and her pink sports socks, and thought about the night when he first made it with her. It was in the laundry room of her building. All the other times they hooked up she looked so scared, like she was in danger of becoming a different person. But that time was just right. They shared a Budweiser, smoked a joint, and listened to some good hip hop beating through the bars of the basement window. She smiled a lot. And the combination of things seemed to make her want to dance a little.

And the basement smelled of bleach, of wetness, of weed, of ratty towels drying over a pipe. There was a rusted sink. A pile of unclaimed socks and tee shirts in a dusty corner. And the darkness. Just one faint lightbulb entertaining moths. And the little wood bench where people sat waiting for their laundry to dry. That's where he asked her to lie down. And she took off her thin gold cross, touched it to her lips, and tucked it inside the pocket of her jeans. And her body felt so small beneath him, a child's body as slight as the width of the bench. And she kissed his neck and she licked his lips. And he told her to relax. And he bent her knees. And she gasped for breath. And she grabbed at his neck. And he knew he could keep going as long as she didn't tell him to stop. And he told her he loved her. And he wouldn't let anything happen.

By early April, L.A.s patchwork rainy season had come and gone. It left pinecones scattered on soggy front lawns, vibrant green shrubs, and a mess of leaves clogging gutters of the Spanish style houses on Kovic's idyllic street in Highland Park. Spring is here, she thought. And from spring she could count less than 58 school days to summer. It was just one more leap, the kind they do so brilliantly in the Olympics.

Feeling restless and lonely, Kovic had agreed to an evening of fun and games with Gordon. He arrived with take-out and they joked in bed about being on the clock, about putting the pedal to the metal—getting off quickly—and hitting the road. They both new Gordon couldn't go home too late if he wanted to keep any pretense of having been at dinner with his work team. In fact, they didn't make it to the bedroom. They started kissing in the hallway, where she revealed her new black lingerie, purchased at Target, but which looked more va-va than its price. They did it breathlessly on the living room couch, Kovic believing that the lingerie was a factor in the evening's success. And like always, Gordon called out her two-syllable name—PIA—like a battle cry in a loud exhalation. He was always sweet and full of compliments after sex, reduced to the mind of an exercised puppy.

How are things at home? Kovic asked, trying to sound casual.

They're pretty much the same. Diane made crème brûlée that was quite tasty the other night.

Did she? Kovic said, bolting toward the bathroom. That must be nice for you, Gordon. Her attempts at sweetening the deal.

Well, no. I'd rather have your crème brûlée.

Yeah, right, she said. Anyway, I make what's her name—Ina Garten's—brownies.

By late May, Ruben started work at the loading dock in Carson at 6 a.m. and was the last one to return the truck at the end of the day. His new boss was Eddie, a joker and a reader, and they traded mysteries and crime stories. Eddie introduced him to new writers and Ruben got hooked on a book by James

Ellroy. He told Eddie he thought he drove by street corners described in the book. No shit, Eddie said, it's hard to tell real life from fiction.

Ruben developed a specialty with flat screens and plasmas. He put them in screening rooms, in dens, in guest houses, and even in kids' rooms. Sometimes the ladies of the house answered the door in slim nightgowns like the ones his mother had sewn in the factory. Sometimes he got shaky when the chained Rottweilers growled low and fierce like scary music, or when the sharp-teethed terriers ran out to the driveway, yapping at the van. And sometimes he felt like he wanted to take a souvenir from the fancy houses: an ashtray, a magazine, a flashlight, a ceramic candy bowl. So, a few times he did.

When the people were nice and not too full of themselves, he'd make the urges go away. But when they were rude, when they slapped him on the back and called him *amigo*, he gave in to those urges. He gave Carolina a bar of expensive soap as a present. When she said how good it smelled, like patches of flowers, Ruben just smiled and said that the people at work gave it to him for doing such a good job. He figured that the clients had tons of soap, enough to wash the dirt off the streets and boulevards of L.A.

The nights were warm enough for a long walk up and over the big hill to Bellevue Park where Kovic started running again. One night around 7:30 she saw Ruben—unmistakable—seated on a bench with his arms across his chest, and a phone up to his ear. And then she saw that his little girl was in his lap, pulling at his sleeve. He had been absent the last month of school and she figured that was it. A balding truancy officer had talked with Kovic and the principal about Ruben's absence. She had vouched for him, saying he was a good kid who probably had to help his family.

She waved to Ruben and he waved back. Flipping his phone closed, he stood up with Sofia in his arms. His shoulders were bare, and Kovic remembered about his tattoo. It was a crude depiction of the devil looking goofier than most devils she'd seen. This one had a goatee like Ruben and ears that pointed down. It was more like a bull about to charge.

Hey, Miss, I didn't know you come here, Ruben said.

I run the track when the weather's warm, she said. It's nice to see you, Ruben.

You must run every day, he joked.

She felt exposed in her civilian clothes, her track shorts and a hint of boob spilling from her tank top. She was no longer Ms. Kovic, she was a woman in her early 40s, running in the park. And there was Ruben's baby, so alive, so real.

Ruben jiggled his girl in his arms. This is my Sofia. Her mami is out with friends, so we're hanging out tonight, he said.

Hello sweetie, Kovic said, surprised by the urge to cradle the little girl in her arms. Then, to Ruben, she said, We missed you in class. But I kind of knew.

Yeah, I know. I'm sorry I got busy with work. So.

So, what's your plan? I mean, what are you going to do now?

I don't know, honestly. I guess I'm doing my life. I work for a TV installation company in East L.A. Been talking to my cousin about the service.

The service?

Yeah, see the world. Then get the Army to pay for school.

Not a bad idea, Kovic said, though she hadn't imagined that path for him. Ruben had always seemed like someone destined to do something in the lime-light, but nothing as regimented or as dangerous as the Army.

Oh. Okay. What about the baby? Kovic asked.

Ruben shrugged. I would miss her, but. Her mother can do it, you know. How's your man Ms. Kovic?

Here we go again with my personal life, she said, tugging on her top to keep her navel from showing.

Now I know you got someone. Everybody's got someone. You can't go alone in this world. Even the toads have princesses to kiss. Something my papi used to say.

I suppose, she said, straightening her top.

C'mon, who's your man? A teacher?

No. He's not a teacher. He's…something else.

Like what? A banker? No. Too conservative. He must be…I know…a rapper.

Yeah, that's it. How'd you guess? He's a rapper. How'd you guess?

I thought about you because this client, she gave me a couple of books, one by Fitzgerald, something about paradise.

Kovic looked at Ruben's jovial face. She realized that there was something about him that had always moved her. The thought shook her so much, she pushed it away.

You were my favorite teacher, Ms. Kovic.

Then, without asking permission, Ruben leaned in and held Kovic's body close to his. She relaxed in his arms and she could smell the clean scent of the baby, and feel the smoothness of Ruben's skin against her cheek. The toddler squirmed in his arms, and Ruben whispered something to Sofia in Spanish. The light was a dreamy purple and the air was warm and dry. The three of them bundled in this embrace, while the joggers moved around the track and the world fell away, made Kovic want to cry.

A few weeks later, Gordon and Kovic went to dinner at a place in Silver Lake where they sat in the back patio enjoying another warm evening and eavesdropping on the chatter of young producers and rising stars. They sipped mojitos and ate designer snacks and talked about a case Gordon had pending. He repeated a familiar story about one of the partners at his firm who was a real jackass. And then Gordon seemed to well up with something important. He nodded his head as if he were practicing what he was about to say, or as if he'd already had a conversation with himself.

What is it, Gordon? You're acting really weird.

Am I? I just want you to know that, well, we're finally ready for Redondo.

What's in Redondo?

Oh, he chuckled. I had the final conversation with Diane.

What do you mean?

Oh, I mean, it's over.

What? What's over?

Me and Diane. The marriage. We're…done.

Kovic looked at him, noticing things she'd never seen before. His thin upper lip, the swollen knuckles, the berth of jowl that had grown under his chin when he stopped cycling because of the hip flexor thing.

I did it, he repeated. I had a sip or two of bourbon, and when she was pulling into the garage last night, I told her.

You ambushed your wife in the garage? Kovic said.

I couldn't wait any longer. I said, well, I said, I had met someone, someone she would really like.

What?

…a good caring person, a teacher. Not a young…you know, not a slutty little actress or any-thing like that. And then I said that our lives—hers and mine—would be better if we lived them separately.

You said all that to Diane? In the garage?

Gordon nodded. I did. Near the storage closet where we keep the Campagnolos.

The what?

The bikes, he said.

Kovic nodded, but she felt detached from her body. Across from her was Gordon, who had always been himself. But now he was cloudy, unrecognizable as he ate his fried calamari with robotic arms.

Kovic gestured to the waiter and ordered another mojito.

Make it two! Gordon smiled, taking her hand. We can finally get a little condo, in Redondo.

Kovic stiffened. A wha?

Gordon nodded. I thought you liked the beach. A guy at my office found one right on the sand for under seven…

A condo? My house is…I like my house. Wait a minute. Wait, Gordon. I thought…

It's got to be the TV, he said.

Kovic sipped her drink. You saw something on TV and decided to dump your wife?

No, no. I finally broke down and got Diane a flatscreen. Yeah, this funny Mexican dude came and installed it last week. Diane's been in heaven ever since. She's stopped cooking, just sits around flipping those channels. Never asks me where I'm going, what I'm doing, who I'm with. She's over me.

Huh, Kovic said, swirling a cube in her mouth.

She said after watching the first season on the flatscreen, she started thinking about gettin' a big D – divorce.

Diane? She asked you for a…?

Isn't that something? All systems go!

Kovic stared into the void.

P?

Pia? Isn't this great?

Hello? Earth to Kovic. Do you read me?

Whisper Language

Los Angeles, 2008

Luke rubs his eyes and reaches for his inhaler.
He takes a long pull off the white valve, starting his
day with a gentle punch to his lungs. He was a pro
when it came to bong hits and Camels. Now, at 38,
he's paying for it. He scratches his belly, adjusts himself in his boxers, and tells me, It's your turn to walk
the dog.

He stares at me plaintively and I stare back,
waiting for someone to make the next move. He'll
be out of the house for good soon enough, so I won't
protest about the dog.

I'm confused by the fact that I still like the
way he looks in the morning, his silvery hair cropped
close to his head like moss. I still like what I see in his
sensual face, the press of his lips.

I throw on my bathrobe and slippers, grab the
leash and a plastic grocery bag, and I'm a ghost wife,
half awake, trailing dutifully after our old Labrador
down Ronda Vista Drive.

I could forgive Luke for the first few years, the moodiness, and the depression. I could file it under *that's just his disease* or it's no mistake who you marry. But the things that happened, the things that I let happen to Ingrid, well, there's no forgiving that.

When it came time to get married, we thought of heading to Vegas, finding one of those drive-through chapels, but my mother arranged for us to wed at my father's golf club in Palos Verdes. And, since I knew she wasn't thrilled with my choice of husband, I didn't want to disappoint her twice.

Luke was in his white, second-hand suit, his flashy tie and his sideburns jutting out beneath his temples. He looked like a racecar driver, cool and fast. I was in the knee-length dress my mom had worn to her own wedding in Healdsburg, California, in 1966. I felt like she must have felt: scared, excited and a little bit giddy.

I took the vows, repeating each word carefully like a prayer. I kept my eyes closed, keeping the sun on my neck like a tonic, and clutching Luke's hand, which was warm and familiar. The two of us stood perfectly still against the cool breeze off the Pacific

Ocean. Two coordinating points fixed on a map of love. I remember thinking *this is how a life together starts: with this much love and good intentions.*

When all our friends drove away, Luke hiked up my dress and we screwed behind the snack bar, laughing and sighing with relief. It felt different having married sex. The thrill had a different notion, like you were destined to do this, meant to do this, until your bodies failed.

That first year we were married I kept thinking please, *no babies yet*, I just want to get used to this. And, months later when my jeans didn't fit over my widening hips and all the common smells in the house felt too thick inside my nose, Luke told me, Look out, Kate, I think a little miracle is coming. And he was right.

Ingrid is an eight-year-old with matted blonde hair down her back and eyes like watery blue ripples in the Caribbean. She's a head taller than all the girls in her class, and she dances throughout the day in Martha Graham-like movements. Starting in kindergarten, we could tell she had *differences.* That was the school director's polite way of saying she wasn't entirely sure if Ingrid would have words that followed her throughout her life. Ingrid is difficult and ethereal, and prone to angry tantrums, even when the other kids her age have found more productive ways to channel their anxieties.

There's much to love about Ingrid. She kisses snails she finds on the curb outside our house after it rains, saying everyone needs a peck. She wears tissue paper and Scotch tape dresses topped by tinfoil crowns, and talks to me in a whisper language she invented that sounds vaguely like a mixture of Russian and French. She draws pictures of boats with silvery wings that fly past the moon, and of Megaworms, weighted down by their own rocket-powered butts. But she can't for the life of her figure out the sum of 2x4. The numbers jumble up like clothes in a dryer and she shakes her wrists as if she's casting off the empty space covering up the answer.

If I could find every sum, every spelling, every lost answer, I'd give it to her. I would. She knows I would.

The last time Luke and I had a real conversation about Ingrid was the day we went to buy some supplies for his studio. We drove over to the Builder's

Supply on San Fernando next to the roller rink where Ingrid and I used to eat grilled cheese sandwiches and pretend to be expert skaters.

Apparently she hides out all day, or she provokes her classmates—out of boredom, I told him. Are you aware that she's been holed up in the back of the classroom all week speaking in that whisper language?

You worry too much about Ingrid, Luke said. Our girl's a little different is all.

He said I made too big a deal about things.

She's just trying to get attention. She'll settle down, he said. Maybe let her have a soda pop once in a while like the other kids. You're like a sugar Nazi.

It bugged me that he called it soda pop. But he was right. Ingrid's progressive school that we could barely afford had sent home a note with a list of items that were okay and not okay. Peanut butter-filled pretzels: okay. Oreos: taboo. I tried to comply but at times it felt restrictive.

Maybe we should think about a different school, I told him, pushing our cart into the massive warehouse.

I don't, he said, rushing ahead of me. Unless it's the public school around the corner.

Then he paused. He had a mean smile. And you should stop spending so much time at the office—that guy you work for doesn't have a family. He doesn't know all the time you spend together is making yours fall apart.

We were becoming strangers who once were best friends, our lives dividing like water when the rudder of the boat passes through. I'd see Luke in his sweats, fooling around on the bass. He'd have a bowl of Cheerios by his side, or he might be zoning out to one of his crime shows like *Law & Order*. And I'd think, this was the guy who got out of his town in Minnesota, moved to L.A., said he'd beat all the odds. This guy, with his crazy-ass dances, his Chevy Malibu with its horn that sounded like a drunken laugh, and his painful jabs about the different types of depression he had in his family. This was the guy who wanted Ingrid so badly he stroked her newborn head like a dove's tail, kissed her miniature cheeks and told her, I'm your Daddy, now. Don't you fly away. The guy who told me he would never do drugs again.

On good days, I saw traces of the young Luke, the one who had ambition enough for all of us. He was going to discover new bands and talked about building a studio up north on some generous piece of land.

We'll live near a river, so we can hear it whispering at night, he'd say. We'll teach Ingrid to fish like a pro. She'll recite the names of trees like the alphabet and learn to sail a boat in all kinds of weather.

If I think back, Luke and I stopped desiring each other and went our separate ways when I started building the house for Clea Taylor. Clea was a 26-year-old actress who bought herself a home in the Los Feliz hills with TV money after landing a lead on *Second Chance*, a right wing show about a group home for teenage girls who decide they're keepin' their babies. She played Jenny, a character described by one entertainment mag as a show about *an 18-year-old caring for her infant son in a cruel but sanitized world*. In real life, Clea has an on-again-off-again relationship with a paunchy British art dealer who tired of his wife when she hit 40, claiming things were getting messy. This is all according to Alana, a friend I've known since college, who inteviewed Clea for a ones-to-watch feature in *Variety*.

I admit that the Clea Taylor project took over. I guess all my projects have a way of doing that. For several months, I worked late hours and became obsessed with small details—countertops, built-ins, and windows that framed the sky, the valley, and the trees. I got loose about the big events that made up my life. I neglected bills and yes, I let the car insurance lapse. I forgot to make the roasted peppers I'd promised for the potluck. I stopped going to the L.A. River meetings, and completely bagged on the book club. Sorry, Meg Wolitzer! And around that time I lost my ambivalence towards Luke. I heard something in an Al-Anon meeting about *detaching with love* and it all made sense. I stopped wondering if we were going to make it. We had gone as far as we could. In fact, I was plotting my escape when I got that shitty phone call from Ingrid's school.

Kate? This is Jackie Powell, Dr. Powell from Lakeview, she said. Ingrid's fine but she attacked another child, someone she said she considers a friend. And there was blood.

I asked if it was someone who makes fun of her. I asked about Clara and another girl.

I can't say the child's name, she said. I think it started out as a game, but I'm afraid this is a little more complicated. I'm hoping you and your husband can come in early tomorrow morning after drop off.

I hung up and looked at young Clea who was half-dressed, inspecting the kitchen tile while drinking her coffee. Her face was softer and kinder than I remembered from a few minutes ago.

Something happen? she asked.

Not really, something with the family, I mumbled.

Oh. Is it your husband?

I guess I had been spilling my guts about the problems I'd been having with Luke. I'd probably said too much about his temper, about his getting loud in restaurants. That's what people do when they're in trouble, when things can no longer be contained. They spill.

Nothing to worry about, I said. I won't be around until the afternoon tomorrow. But, the cabinets are arriving tomorrow and I'd say we're in good shape, I told her.

Sure, she said, smiling with her good girl teeth. Let me know if I can do anything.

She smiled at me like she was a friend, someone who trusted me to fix problems and make things right. The grown up in the room. I stared at her blankly. I didn't know how to tell her that my child was violent and I was afraid of the short drive home.

Ingrid's school was on a big piece of land with the Pasadena freeway churning in the background. The main buildings were designed by one of my favorite architects, and it has always given me a quiet thrill to walk the campus. I was so grateful that Ingrid was awarded a scholarship here. The director's office is in a tidy bungalow, slightly removed from the action. As I approached her door, my whole body felt tight, like a rope had been wrapped around my insides.

Dr. Powell was a tall woman with a serene, inviting face. She was there at the door, with her long arms, the dark color of branches, stretched out to hug me. But just after the hug, she composed herself and began to speak like the seasoned administrator she was.

The game was rather difficult to play, she said. Ingrid forced the other child to pick up some food off the ground and eat it. Ingrid pointed to some raisins and celery sticks that had fallen from the other child's lunch box. The child refused at first, but apparently Ingrid scolded her and told her that she had to eat them, or Ingrid would stop being her friend.

Did you see this? How do you know this happened? I asked, hoping an unseen element might have provoked some of Ingrid's aggression.

The other child kept refusing to eat the last few raisins on the ground, so Ingrid told her that no one would ever speak to her again. She'd be cast off with no friends to comfort her. I guess she meant no one in the class. The child threw some raisins and pebbles at Ingrid, and that's when Ingrid got very agitated and scratched the child's neck, and bit her on the shoulder.

God, I'm sorry.

The child who was bitten was crying for quite some time after she was bandaged, Dr. Powell said, so we moved into a Conflict Room with the lead teacher before the parents came and took her to the pediatrician.

This did not sound like Ingrid, but it was Ingrid. Sweet and savage Ingrid. This was her act of war, learned at home, conceived with malice, carried out with precision. And the other one, the poor child on the receiving end. What had she done to deserve this?

This is hard to imagine, I managed.

I know, said Dr. Powell, quieter now, about to deliver the final blow. Kate, I'm sorry that your husband couldn't make it. We need to talk with him as well. Ingrid said something else in the Conflict Room. She said that you and Luke had scared her the other night. She said you guys had an argument.

We were angry at each other, but I didn't think—

She said you or your husband—it wasn't clear—dragged her roughly—to the kitchen. She said her Daddy banged her wrist. Something about the sink.

God. No, he didn't...

She showed us a bruise.

Evidence, I thought. *A report.* Something happened to Ingrid.

If it was something... It was an accident, I said.

Were you angry at Ingrid? Dr. Powell asked, looking through me.

No, no. I was angry with Luke for—we're having problems. I mean, we're separating soon, but

I haven't—Ingrid woke up and she started crying and complaining that she wanted water, and she wouldn't stay in her room.

Dr. Powell's kinder tone was gone. Nothing conciliatory now. Did you take her to the kitchen, she asked, in a forceful way?

I talked to to her teacher about it. There have been some arguments in the house.

Okay. But I have to ask you again, did you hurt Ingrid?

I hesitated and then I said: I thought this was about the biting. We can talk to her about the biting.

Initially, I thought this was about the biting incident, too, said Dr. Powell, whose face had shifted like the sky when a storm is about to pass through.

Please, I said, as images from that night came rushing to me like a blurry crime scene. I didn't mean to get Ingrid involved in our fight. I would never—we would never hurt her.

Dr. Powell shifted her body to face me directly. I know. I know that.

Then she put her arms around me as I wept. Sound was gone. Breath was gone. I wondered how

I had gotten onto the freeway, to the school, to the path, to this room where I buried my face in the crook of her neck. Poor Ingrid, I thought, with her power play, her bag of evil tricks. And her bruise, worn like a pale purple bracelet on her wrist.

Dr. Powell stood up, signaling that we were done.

We have to listen when a child tells us she's been injured by someone close to her, she said, her face tightening as she whispered. We have no choice.

On the drive back to the house, I felt small and raw and full of shame. I thought of how things would have escalated if Luke had been there. I thought of who we were and who we'd been.

When we first met, Luke played bass in a local L.A. band called The Other Digit, while struggling with a little coke problem; he's been in and out of *the rooms* since he was 20. This doesn't make him a bad person, but it does make him that person.

Some people get all the luck, leaving nothing but a sorry pair of dice for the rest of us, he'd say when things weren't going his way. He got that idea from his father, a transportation manager and amateur photographer in Columbia Heights, Minnesota who blew all his pension at the track, and then blew half his head off—when Luke was 14—while his wife was asleep in the next room.

I guessed at being a good wife half the time, and I suppose I never made my peace with the idea that my career as an architect would have to mean so much less than all of this. Confessions: 1) My firm sent us to a conference in Paris and I flew there with two handsome colleagues just 10 weeks after Ingrid was born. I drank cheap chablis on the plane and flirted like a sexed-up teen who had escaped from boarding school. *Slutty Kate the Infidel.*

I didn't cry until I got back to my hotel room with my achy boobs that barely had a shot at feeding the little one. I rang one of my colleagues and he came by with iced martinis.

Last year, I missed the Valentine's Day party at Ingrid's school because I had to drive to Santa Monica to oversee a screw-up on a guesthouse we were doing. When I got home that night, Ingrid showed me a heart-shaped card out of tinfoil. It said *I love you, mommy* in crackly, green glue.

Do you like the heart I made you? Ingrid whispered, as I bathed her long, perfect body later that night. *It has a secret chamber just for you.*

When I told Ingrid that her Daddy was moving out, Ingrid had her questions. That was all she had. She understood that there would be an undoing, and maybe she'd use the answers I gave to glue the pieces back in place.

If we all live in a different house, will you still be my parents?

We'll both be your parents, I said. You'll get to have two homes, I guess—one with Daddy and one with me.

She continued, burrowing deeper into the truth, calculating the odds, and drawing a picture of what she was in for.

Will I have a the pink flamingo lamp next to my bed at the new house?

Will Slim (the parakeet) or Rosy (the Labrador) live with us in the new house?

Will you and daddy ever live in the same house again?

I looked at my daughter from my rear view

mirror. The ends of her feathery blond hair were pasted to the worn leather seat of the Volvo; her cheeks were as pale and shiny as an eggshell. The questions kept coming like the rectangular white footprints of the freeway, the strange, modern hieroglyphs that keep us all moving in the same direction. In the distance were the proud peaks of the San Gabriel Mountains.

And then she called out the question that I was afraid to ask: If you loved Daddy, how could your love just blow away?

A few weeks later, after stiff conversations and periods of murderous silence, Luke started to move his things out. In truckloads, he took his amps, his bass, some photos of Ingrid, and some of his clothes, a box of crime novels and a book by Bukowski I gave him one year. Each time he pulled away in the pickup, the neighbors took note, and I waved good-bye from the front porch steps.

See ya, Katie, he said.

He said it as if I were what? Someone he knew.

Luke moved in with his brother in Highland Park. He started back to the meetings he liked, the ones held in the back room of the bakery. He sounded good last time we spoke. Though I'm not sure I know what good Luke really sounds like. Besides, I'm learning that how he sounds, what he does, it's not my business.

Sunday morning after breakfast, I take Ingrid to Matador Beach, a coastal spot where we used to go for fun when we first moved to L.A. Ingrid twirls down the long flight of steps on ballerina legs. She's in her red bikini and striped flip-flops, a ponytail sprouting from her head. Her skinny arms carry a beach bag with her favorite SpongeBob towel. I'm behind her dragging the cooler, inching my way down, welcoming the heat of the sun on my face, and the breeze coming off the ocean. Feeling free of the story of Luke, the worry, the hurt.

Where should we put our towels down? Ingrid asks, scouting a spot that is not too far from the water.

I tell her, We'll go where we always go.

You mean where we used to go with Daddy?

Near the cave, past the tide pools, I say.

Daddy doesn't really like the beach that much, you know.

For a moment, I think about the times I dragged Luke here, hung-over, to slump in a patch of shade.

He still gets mad a lot, Ingrid says, jumping into the sand off the last step. Then he's sorry. Sometimes I miss when he lived in the house with us. And sometimes I don't, she says.

Me, too, I say, trying to catch up with her interpretive leaps and dashes across the beach.

This is our spot, Ingrid says, dropping the towels and flinging off her flip-flops near a huddle of giant rocks. Clara says oceans were once ice cubes. Is that true?

Sort of, I answer, wishing I knew so much more about the natural world. There were these huge glaciers that covered the earth. When they melted, this is what was left, the ocean.

Cool, Ingrid says. When the ice comes back, we can put on our skates and skate all over the world.

I hand her the sunscreen and she pours a big white glob into her hand.

Mom?

Yeah?

That lady whose house you built, does she have a kid?

Only on television. Why?

So, she pretends to know all that stuff about babies?

Right, I say. It's all make-believe.

Oh, Ingrid says.

She mushes the cream into my leg and draws a face. This makes her laugh. Then she buries her peach pit in the sand, making a hidden treasure.

You told the school that Daddy hurt me, didn't you? Ingrid draws in the sand. A sun. A moon.

Why do you say that? I ask.

Ingrid gets up, impatient.

Because of what the social worker lady said. She made me tell her about the night that I got scared and hurt my wrist. She asked me if it ever happened before.

Oh, I said. And what did you say?

I don't know.

Okay.

I told her that the hurting did happen once with Daddy. Not with you. I told her about the time in the park when he got frustrated and I fell on the ground and scraped my knee. How I peeked underneath the Band-aid every day.

I touch her soft pink arm. I promise that won't happen anymore, I say.

Ingrid nods. Let's go in the water, mama! she says, shaking the sand off her towel. She walks in ahead of me, letting the ocean wrap around her ankles. She takes a few more steps and I watch until she is half-emerged in a skirt of soft white foam. Then she turns and waves.

She is a beautiful child with secrets and imperfections. A child who will grow up learning how the waves of the Pacific Ocean break in unexpected patterns, whispering as they flatten over rocks and sand—only to gather strength and form anew.

With Gratitude

This book would not have happened without the creative vision of Ruth Höflich and the folks at 8fold Occasional Press. Thank you to my Editor, Connie Pearson, for your insightful and generous gifts. To Alison Dickey, Kim Bender, Emily Karaszewski, Jocelyn Heaney, Ina Imbrey and Carol Schwartz for championing these stories. Thank you to writer-mentors, Rob Roberge, Dana Johnson, and Jim Krusoe, for helping me shape this collection. Antonio, my gratitude for believing in all my writing endeavors, especially this one. Deep love to Gala + Cassio for inspiring me to carry on.

Photography and book design by Ruth Höflich.
Ruth is a visual artist working in moving image, photography and print.

ISBN: 968-0-578-38548-8

Deirdre Mendoza is a journalist whose stories and essays have been published in *Ms.com*, *The Los Angeles Times*, *WWD*, *Variety*, and *The Miami New Times*. She holds an MFA from Antioch University, L.A., and teaches writing at Glendale College and Woodbury University.

All photography © 2022 by Ruth Höflich
Published by 8fold Occasional Press, 2021

CPSIA information can be obtained
at www.ICGtesting.com
Printed in the USA
LVHW020717150622
721315LV00010B/517

9 780578 385488